Inner Bridges

Inner Bridges

A Guide to Energy Movement
And Body Structure

Fritz Frederick Smith, M.D.

HUMANICS NEW AGE
Atlanta, Georgia

Revised Second Printing 1994

Bridge illustrations by Jean Piccioulo.
Cover illustration by Mauro Magellan.

PRINTED IN THE UNITED STATES OF AMERICA

Library of Congress Cataloging in Publication Data

Smith, Fritz Frederick, 1929–
Inner Bridges.
Includes bibliographies and index.
1. Medicine, Oriental — Philosophy. 2. Mind and body.
3. Vitality. I. Title. [DNLM: 1. Anatomy. 2. Energy.
3. Medicine, Oriental Traditional. 4. Movement.
WB 50.1 S 647i]
R 581.S 55 1986 613 86-2899
ISBN 0-89334-086-3

Humanics Limited
P.O.Box 7400
Atlanta, Georgia 30309

To my parents,
Margaret Reindel Smith
and
Ernest J. Smith, D.C.

Inner Bridges is not a how-to-do-it book. Exercise and balancing techniques are given specifically to illustrate ideas under discussion. They are not intended for clinical instruction of the reader.

Acknowledgments

I wish to thank Julia Measures who first motivated me to share information; Myrtle Bradley and Susan and Steve James for encouraging me to write; Gary Wilson for making the book possible; Jody Bailey, Cheryle Dembe Brunner, Aminah Raheem, Ed Chin, Roy Capellaro, Terry Brickley, Jim McCormick, and Gary Dolowich for their constant support and encouragement; Sandy and Jim Handley for their review of the first manuscript; Susan Sparrow and Hal Zina Bennett for their help with style and content; Carol Riddle for her illustrations and Jean Picciuolo for her bridge drawings; Lori Annaheim and Linda Benefield for their editorial help; my wife Betty for her clarity of judgment and vision. Finally, I want to extend special thanks to my many friends, patients, and teachers who have shared in my journey.

Contents

Introduction

It is my hope in writing this book that I might make a contribution to the expanding vision of the human body as an integrated system. Specifically, I want to explore the connections or bridges that exist between the seen and unseen elements of the human body. To that end, *Inner Bridges* expresses my belief that "energy" exists as a specific force, with its own anatomy, physiology, and pathophysiology. It is my conviction, backed by experience, that this energy force, once accepted and experienced, can alter our view of nature and, in the process, aid us in maintaining health and in overcoming disease.

I grew up in a family that was involved with science and health practice, and I was educated in the scientific community. I received a B.A. in Zoology and Chemistry, was trained as an Osteopathic Physician and Surgeon (1955), and received an M.D. in 1961. Seventeen years of active general practice followed. Then my entire understanding of human health and illness was challenged and ultimately expanded.

For a long time I had felt that my medical understanding could not account for things I had experienced regarding the human body and healing. I could not identify what was missing, but knew that somewhere there were explanations. In the mid 1960s I explored different areas including cranial osteopathy, clinical hypnosis, and structural integration (Rolfing), while searching for that information. I had formative insights and experiences, but none so powerful or profound that I could not ignore or "bend" what I had learned to fit my scientific view of reality. However, in 1971, within two days of my introduction to Traditional Chinese Acupuncture and the teachings of Professor J.R. Worsley, my scientific model cracked. I observed events, some recounted in this book, that I could not explain or incorporate into my medical understandings. As a result, the foundations of my scientific model shifted, and an expanded view of nature came to life.

My medical information was not incorrect, but was limited and constrained by the empirical method, the demand for proof, for tangibility, for causal relationships, for facts. Everything I had been taught up to that point ignored the intuitive and experiential side of life. It taught illness as an *event* and not as a *process* taking place within the broader scope of a person's life. It did not recognize the tacit and intrinsic concept of "energy" and the world of inherent movement, which have long been acknowledged in Eastern philosophy and other healing systems. I had accepted my medical model as the full story; now I knew it was only one chapter of the much broader subject of health, wholeness, and human potential.

I became a serious student, experiencer, practitioner, and eventually teacher of the use of "energy" in healing. My pivotal influence was J.R. Worsley, through his College of Chinese Acupuncture in England (1971–78), where I earned my license of acupuncture, Bachelor of Acupuncture, and Master of Acupuncture degrees. I later became a faculty member of The Traditional Acupuncture Institute, Columbia, Maryland. I have been a student of Jack Schwartz and Brugh Joy; have studied Jin Shin Do and Shiatsu; have explored meditation, yoga, T'ai Chi Chuan, and Chi Kung. In my clinical practice I began to integrate the world of inherent movement and energy with my scientific skills and understanding. During this process I came to recognize a specific area in a person where movement and structure are in juxtaposition, similar to the situation in a sailboat where the wind (movement) and the sail (structure) meet. From the explanation of this interface, in 1973 I formulated the structural acupressure system of Zero Balancing to evaluate and balance the relationship between energy and structure. The effects I have seen in people following Zero Balancing sessions have led me to understand that the bridging of energy and matter exists in the level of the body and the mind and the spirit of a person, and that any or all of these levels can be addressed.

The implications of my understanding and experience of the structural/energetic interface led me to dissolve a successful general medical practice, specialize in the broader field of health, wellness, and human potential, and teach basic principles of structure and energy which I have encountered. *Inner Bridges* is a further manifestation of this journey, which has literally involved thousands of patients.

This book is not a how-to book. Rather, it is a treatise examining the connections between ancient theories of energy and modern medicine, between Eastern esoteric anatomy and Western human anatomy, between subjective *inner experience* and objective observation. It speculates on the nature of energy physiology and pathophysiology, and on energy imbalances as they relate to our modern understanding of Western physiology. In addition, *Inner Bridges* explores the growing relationship between Western medicine and the alternative health care system in this country, hoping these bridges will establish better communication and understanding in both directions.

The thoughts and ideas expressed in this book are a point of view, and a report of the life experiences of one physician, which I hope will enhance or challenge the reader's understanding of energy as related to the human body. The appreciation and understanding of energy is rapidly expanding, and my goal is not to establish a scientific argument for these beliefs, but to stimulate the reader to reflect on his or her personal experience. With the growing complexity of our world we need to share our knowledge and create a greater rather than lesser number of options. If the reader glimpses a new potential or possibility in these pages, this book will have served its purpose, adding to the ever-widening vision of the human body and its potential.

1

Bridging Belief Systems

"The map is not the territory."

As we each develop in our personal lives, we consciously and unconsciously create inner views or "mental models" of the universe that become a part of who we are. Most of us know this phenomenon as "building a belief system." As we move through life, this model or belief system is continually challenged. In order to maintain our physical, mental, and spiritual health, we must successfully adapt to these challenges and assimilate new information. Much of what we experience concurs with our model, thus supporting what we already know, or helping us to take our knowledge a step further. The educational system and cultural programming augment this process. However, there are experiences in our lives which seem contrary to our belief systems or completely new to them. When we encounter such experiences, we have the choice of altering our models to accommodate the new information, rationalizing the new data to make it fit our existing model, or ignoring the information by pretending it did not happen or does not exist. Events that challenge our belief systems and ultimately cause us to change our views, thereby decreasing our attachment to previous beliefs, are truly formative events in our lives. They offer new potentials.

The mental model or belief system is a theoretical construct that organizes information and experiences, but never quite represents things "the way they really are." The model is not the reality; the map is not the territory. Yet this model of the world directly shapes our response to "reality," and is so deeply ingrained that the process of changing maps, or letting go of existing belief systems, is usually a struggle filled with uncertainty and pain.

Eastern Philosophy In the Western World

In the field of medicine and healing, one of the most recent challenges to our cultural viewpoint has been the introduction of Eastern philosophy into the Western world. In Western scientific traditions we are asked to objectively analyze data and events external to ourselves; in the Eastern tradition we are asked to subjectively investigate the internal world through contemplation, meditation, and body control. The conclusions and constructs from Eastern traditions provide models of reality that are very different from those of the West—or at least so it seems on the surface. Fritjof Capra, Ph.D., in his book, *Tao of Physics,* makes an eloquent case for the fact that the further Western science delves into the world of particle and subatomic physics, the more the conclusions drawn begin to look like those reached through ancient Eastern meditative practices.

A key premise in Eastern thinking is the existence of "energy." For thousands of years this has been conceived as a specific force; in China it is referred to as *Ch'i*; In Japan it is *ki*; and in India it is *prana*. Within recent Western scientific history there have been pioneers such as Samuel Hahnemann, Friedrich Mesmer, the Rev. C.W. Leadbeater and Wilhelm Reich, [1] to mention a few, who have worked with "energy" as a healing entity. The work of these men went so far outside the model of mainstream Western medical thinking that it initially

[1] Samuel Hahnemann (1755 – 1843) A German physician, founder of Homeopathy.
Friedrich Mesmer (1733 – 1815) A German physician, postulated a magnetic force ("animal magnetism"), teacher of hypnosis (mesmerize).
Rev. Charles W. Leadbeater (1847 – 1934) Vice-rector of the Church of England, student of yoga, author of approximately thirty books, including *Chakras* (1927).
Wilhelm Reich, M.D. (1897 – 1957) A protege of Freud, discoverer of "orgone energy."

won them little more than ridicule, accusations of quackery, and even imprisonment.

Acupuncture Analgesia

The Western medical community was again confronted with the issue of "energy" in 1972, in the form of acupuncture analgesia. I was present at Stanford University on June 14, 1972, when the Academy of Parapsychology, in conjunction with the American Medical Association convention in San Francisco, presented a day-long program on acupuncture. President Nixon had recently opened the doors to China, and James Reston had had his now famous appendectomy using acupuncture for postsurgical pain control. Many excellent speakers came to the platform that day at Stanford, speaking about acupuncture theory and practice to an audience of more than 1300 doctors and nurses. There was a restlessness in the audience that morning, and a general sense of disbelief as the acupuncture model was being presented. The information seemed foreign and irrelevant to those whose training was limited to the Western concept of health and disease.

The most dramatic moment came after the lunch break when films were shown of surgeries being performed. A cancerous lung was removed, the only anesthesia being an acupuncture needle in each of the patient's ears and another in each arm, manually stimulated by the attending acupuncturist. The film showed a patient having a brain tumor excised with the aid of an acupuncture needle inserted in the forearm. Surgery after surgery was documented in the film, all with the use of acupuncture as the analgetic agent. In some cases, the acupuncturists were manipulating the needles, in others the needles were stimulated by a machine delivering a low voltage current. Throughout each procedure the patients were awake, talking, and even occasionally taking sips of water. At the conclusion of one surgery the patient sat up on the table and shook hands with his doctor and the attending staff. In another case, after the removal of a thyroid tumor, the patient actually stepped down from the operating table and walked to the wheelchair by himself.

As the film ended and the lights came up, the auditorium at Stanford was as still as a church. There was not a sound from the audience; the atmosphere was one of intense calm and awe, the mood almost reverent. People had just witnessed a series of events that were totally outside their model of reality. During the intermission that followed, individual responses to the material in the film ranged from fascination to total incredulity. One doctor suggested the movie was a fake and a mock-up, a propaganda tool from The People's Republic of China. Fortunately, Paul Dudley White, M.D., renowned cardiologist, was a participant in the panel discussion that followed. He had been to China as a member of the team of doctors who had filmed the surgeries just presented. He fully corroborated what the audience had just seen in the film.

Even now, thirteen years later, after many of us have been to China and witnessed these procedures with our own eyes, the deep implications of the analgetic feat of acupuncture has yet to be fully grasped. The fact that acupuncture analgesia does in fact work has fundamentally challenged our physiologic and medical models and has resulted in extensive research to explain the mechanism of the phenomenon.

The Scientific Community Responds

Since the advent of acupuncture analgesia, research centers the world over have been engaged in an intense, exciting race to find a rational explanation for what makes acupuncture effective in pain control. These efforts have fostered numerous beneficial offshoots including the development of transcutaneous stimulators for self pain control; electrical stimulation to promote tissue healing; and the discovery of the endorphin group of chemical compounds, the natural morphine-like substance produced in our bodies. Pain control clinics have developed, biofeedback has expanded, and paranormal phenomena have attracted new interest.

A less spectacular, but truly significant, ramification has been the mushrooming interest in acupuncture as a general form of therapy, beyond its pain control properties. Serious study of this ancient healing system has become a bridge into Eastern philosophies and the realm of Traditional Chinese Medicine. Sufficient interest has been sparked to translate classic oriental texts and modern writings concerning the theory and practice of acupuncture, herbology, meditation, and the martial arts. The bridge between ancient and modern China is filled with activity; individuals, professionals, and whole cultures are moving more freely across it.

As the exchange of acupuncture information and research continues, there is a growing agreement in the Western medical community that acupuncture and Traditional Chinese Medicine have credibility. Despite the ongoing research, however, to my knowledge, not one scientific theory has yet surfaced to satisfactorily explain *all* the effects seen with acupuncture analgesia and acupuncture therapy.

Energy as an Observable Experience

One of the elusive principles of acupuncture centers in the understanding of *ch'i*, the vital life force. Its nature has not yet yielded to studies based on the scientific method, although it can be experienced on a personal level in such profound ways that there can be little doubt of its existence. Through the study of acupuncture and body therapy, and the actual objective and subjective appreciation of energy moving in the physical body, it seems that *ch'i* exists as a specific and significant force in the body. Its behavior follows general laws that can be identified throughout nature. It can move in currents, with a specific velocity and direction, or may exist as a standing wave form, or as an undefined vibratory field.

If we incorporate "energy" into our view of nature and the human body, fundamental shifts in our perceptions begin to occur. In health and human potential, a multitude of new options and alternative ways of understanding the phenomenal world are possible. In medicine, the acceptance of an energy force such as *ch'i* helps to account for occurrences such as spontaneous healings which are outside of the scientific framework. In psychology and parapsychology the energy force offers an explanation for mental telepathy, materialization, and the special "powers" described in many of the yoga texts. Without the concept of energy some observable phenomena are inexplicable and seem to defy natural law. A prime example of this is firewalking.

Firewalking Tests Our Belief Systems

In 1976, at the Mandala Holistic Health Conference in San Diego, Vernon Craig demonstrated his ability to firewalk. Approximately a thousand people gathered on a golf course to watch him walk over twenty feet of red-hot coals. The commentator, Norman Sheeley, M.D., announced that if there were any doctors present who cared to examine Mr. Craig before and after the firewalk they were welcome to do so. I was one of six physicians who performed an on-the-spot evaluation.

Mr. Craig, wearing a suit and tie, was a slightly overweight, middle-aged man with his pants legs rolled up to his knees. He had normal distribution of hair on his legs. His feet were soft, pliable, completely callus-free, and of normal temperature and texture.

Mr. Craig spoke to the audience, saying that it would take him a few moments to "prepare" to walk on the coals, and that when he was ready he would raise his hand as a signal that he would begin the firewalk. In preparation, Mr. Craig paced back and forth across one end of the fire pit, sipping a cola drink and smoking cigarettes. After a period of thirty minutes or more, he went to the microphone and said that because of the noise from the adjacent freeway, he was having trouble concentrating, and he asked for our patience. Another thirty minutes passed as he smoked more cigarettes and drank another cola. Craig returned to the microphone and told the audience that he was still having difficulty getting "deep enough" and although at that moment was able to walk the coals without pain, he was afraid that his feet would burn and blister if he tried. Sensing the restlessness of the crowd, he said that he would be willing to do this, but was interrupted by Dr. Sheeley who would permit Craig to complete the firewalk only if he felt he could do so without injury. At that point someone from the audience offered to loan Mr. Craig a set of ear plugs to help him block out the freeway noise. After inserting the plugs in his ears, Craig indicated his satisfaction and again began pacing across the end of the pit. Several minutes later he raised his arm and proceeded to walk the twenty feet across the bed of burning coals.

Immediately after the walk we reexamined him. He seemed tired but otherwise fine. His facial color was slightly pale and there was dampness on his forehead. His feet had ashes on them, but they were cool to the touch, slightly sweaty, and free from any signs of burns or blisters or redness that might indicate irritation. They were not even tender to the touch. Years ago I had read accounts and seen pictures of ceremonies where people in states of hysteric frenzy or deep trance walked on coals. In this past year I have read of workshops in this country where the average person is empowered to walk on coals after a program of a few hours in learning to "overcome fear." As impressive as these reports are, however, it was when I witnessed Mr. Craig calmly walking across this field of glowing embers that the immensity of the accomplishment struck me. My prior experiences and mental model told me that human tissue burns when subjected to high temperatures. Even though I have experienced that this is not necessarily true, my mind still struggles to understand which law or principle of nature allows for this possibility. The closest I have come to an explanation is to postulate that a person can alter the vibrations of the body to match or exceed the vibrations of the burning coals or to refine them so the heat vibration will actually pass through the body; in either case becoming "immune" to burning.

The following morning Mr. Craig spoke to a general audience. He disclosed that his ability to firewalk, along with his ability to control pain, stop bleeding, and increase the healing rates of his body tissue came as a result of working with principles outlined in Yoga Ramacharaka's book, *Advanced Course in Yoga Philosophy and Oriental Occultism.* The basic teaching involved breath control, the one system of the body where we have voluntary control over an involuntary function. Through this bridge to the autonomic nervous system and energy systems of his body, Mr. Craig mastered paranormal abilities, including walking on fire, without injury. Events such as this challenge the Western physiology model at a basic level.

Phenomena which seem *extraordinary* or *paranormal* have been observed by people throughout the ages, and have been documented in so many cultures that the occurrence of these events can hardly be questioned. However, the techniques and beliefs which foster these talents and empower individuals to perform extraordinary feats are as varied as the cultures from which they arise. Yet one common thread runs among them — some concept of a force or energy that transcends the mundane understanding of the physical body.

Bringing Energy Theory into Everyday Life

Spectacular demonstrations of energy control may challenge our existing models of "how things are" and point out discrepancies between our personal experience and analytic thinking. At a more ordinary level, the conceptualization and first-hand knowledge of energy is commonplace in our daily lives, as is reflected even in our everyday vocabulary. Expressions like "I'm running out of steam," "I'm at a low ebb," "I feel high," and "my spirit is low" are all related to our own experiences of our energy fields.

In addition to energy awareness, there are direct experiences of energy itself. Some people perceive its presence more easily than others, but the ability to perceive it is inherent in everyone. Perception of energy is enhanced by the person's acceptance that it *does* exist. This perception is aided by breathing exercises and stilling one's mind through techniques such as mind control, meditation, or contemplation. When the mind is quiet, subtle aspects of our nature become apparent: we sense the "humming," "tingling," or "buzzing" within our bodies; we see the energy field surrounding another person; or we experience the space taken up by our bodies beyond the obvious physical limits.

One way to directly experience energy is to receive acupuncture treatment. The feelings of energy activated by acupuncture are known as *di chi*, which include feelings of a deep ache at the acupuncture site, or a tingling which courses through the body. It is doubly illuminating to look at a classical acupuncture chart, and realize that the exact locations of the tingling you feel can be predicted in energy meridians plotted nearly 2500 years ago. The tingling is not random but follows well-defined paths.

Other healing practices such as acupressure, homeopathy, body work, and creative imagery also yield energetic insights. On the personal level, deep insight of our subtle energy nature can be gained through the martial arts, yoga, or a meditation practice. People have profound experiences of energy during extraordinary stress, as in extremes of ecstasy or near-death experiences. Others become aware of it during altered states of consciousness, during certain types of fasting, in conjunction with prolonged aerobic exercises, during sensory deprivation, and in the use of some mind-altering drugs. Still others experience it through conscious awareness of the struggles and joys of the life process itself.

Toward a Model of Body Energy

As working models of this subtle aspect of the body evolve, care must be taken that they are in accord with natural law. They must also be consistent with our personal world view and flexible enough to change with new information. To be useful in the healing arts, they need to account for diversity, and yet be simple enough to allow for clarity of mind. The model I describe in the following pages has been constructed with these parameters in mind.

Working Energy Model: Particle and Wave

From the broadest viewpoint everything is a form of energy, or, as the Chinese might say, everything is a form of *ch'i*. However, to develop a working model of energy we need to define specific components so that relationships can exist and phenomena occur; to consider the whole in terms of its parts. One fundamental division is that of the particle and the wave. Modern physics has shown that in terms of light, energy can exist as both a particle and a wave, and that these two forms are interchangeable. From the experiential viewpoint, we not only can experience nature in terms of particle (form and structure) and the wave (movement and vibration), but can also experience the *interface* where they meet—standing in a strong wind, leaning into a tree, or at any interface where movement meets form.

Movements of air and water help define and clarify the relationship between the particle and the wave on the level of our sensory perception. Both water and air are media through which waves or currents of energy move. We see the effects of such movements in the forms taken by the particle in those environments. For example, the particles which make up the famous Monterey cypress trees along the coast of central California look as though they are still being blown by a strong wind even on a calm windless day. (See diagram below.) Over the years, as they have grown, the constant blowing from the ocean has caused the branches to take that permanent shape. The tree has become an imprint of the movement of energy.

Monterey Cypress Tree

A more complex example of the relationship betwen the particle and the wave is found in oceanography. The water in the ocean can be considered as an undefined force field which is organized into specific energy currents by outside forces. Within the mass movement of water particles there exist layers of energy that remain relatively stable over long periods of time. Layers of water of different temperatures exist in a stable state, side by side, for many years. Other layers have a specific continuity through which sonar signals can travel for thousands of miles, and in these strata mammals such as the whales can communicate over these long distances.

Any single molecule of water is directly subject to the influence of a diverse number of forces, and can be part of different energy patterns at the same time. Along the California coast, the Japanese current is moving in a southerly direction parallel to the coast. At the same time, the ocean is rising and falling according to tides that are dictated by the moon. The water is influenced by waves moving in a horizontal plane towards the coast. It is also affected by movements of fish and inanimate objects, by stationary objects, and the tortuous configurations of the ocean floor. A single molecule of water can be involved with all these forces simultaneously. The mathematical resolution of these influences is beyond the capability of our most sophisticated computer. Yet, despite the complexity of these various influences, nature resolves these relationships of particle and wave into a totally harmonic system.

Tracing Energy Paths Within the Human Body

In the human body, there is great complexity of energy movement, currents, and vibrations. As in the ocean, body energy can exist freely, in layers, or in organized flows that maintain their integrity and have little tendency to mix. Energy can be blocked, flow freely, or vary in frequency of vibration; it can be in excess or deficient in quantity; and it can be of varying quality.

Body energy, as such, has an anatomy and physiology uniquely its own, separate from the physical body. The anatomy is formed and influenced by the physical structure and its physiology is directly responsive to our thoughts and emotions. It can be experienced, perceived, and altered from within or from outside the body, and is sensitive to environmental and physical forces. This energy takes form in the body in three general ways:

Background Energy Field — First is the all pervasive, diffuse, non-organized vibration which permeates the whole body. It is responsive to forces surrounding and passing through it, but has no form of its own. It can be considered the vibratory backdrop or background music of the body.

Vertical Energy Flows — Second, the body itself acts as a conduit or channel for energy passing through us, the configurations of the body molding that energy into specific forms.

Internal Energy Flows — Third, energy will circulate as currents within the body, with identifiable paths and patterns.

The Working Energy Model

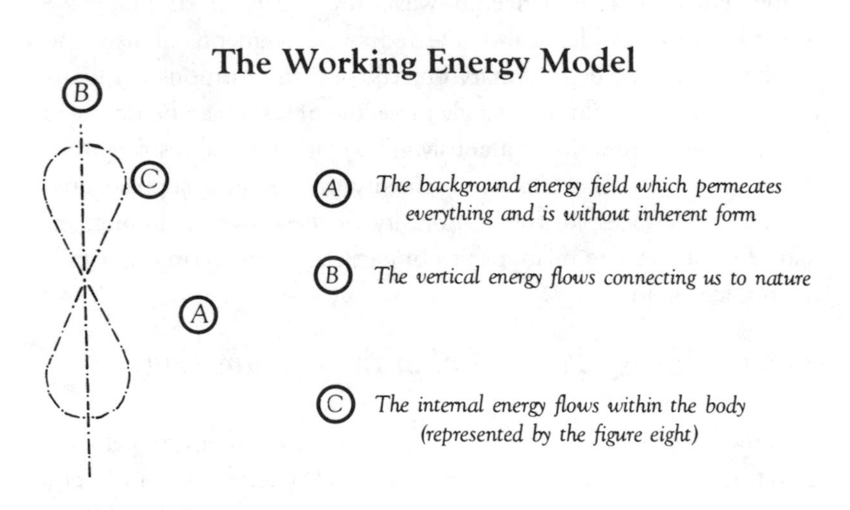

Background Energy Field

This all-pervasive force field has no form of its own, but represents a vibrating field of potential in and about the body. It responds from moment to moment to the internal and external environment of the body, and is directly responsive to our thoughts and emotions and our physical movements. Mild stimulations pass through the field as a wave; major stimulations may leave an imprint in their wake. This field tends to mirror the physical body. It is not an exact mirror, however, since that would imply a static situation and a lack of responsiveness. Instead, there is a reciprocal relationship: any change in either structure or the vibration will affect the other. If a person has a low vibration in this field, he or she appears to be "without starch," tends to slump, and lacks vibrance.

This diffuse field extends beyond the limit of the body structure. How far this vibration extends varies from person to person and changes in response to the health and state of excitation. If one puts one's hand next to a person's body, one will feel the warmth of the heat given off, and as the hand is brought further away, the heat diminishes to a point where it is no longer apparent. Heat is one form of energy, and it requires no stretch of the imagination to say that the heat emanating from a person's body is one expression of that person's vibratory field. In addition to the heat emanations, a number of more subtle vibrations together constitute the "aura" or "auric field."

There are a number of people who are sensitive to the vibrations of the aura, who can not only see it around another person but can describe its color, its dimension, its layers, and even see holes and gaps within the emanation. A "sensitive" person can give an "aura reading" telling about events in our personal history, and can administer healing through balancing and harmonizing these emanations. Other people can hear the gentle hum or buzz of this field, while others can feel its density.

Vertical Energy Flows

To exist as separate beings, to be manifest on the material plane as we are, we must be both a *part* of the fabric of nature and independent of it. This dual requirement determines two basic energy flows in our bodies: one conducts energy through the body and connects us with nature; the other relates to the circulation of energy within the body and organizes us as individuals.

Every upright object, whether animate or inanimate, acts as an antenna or lightning rod, conducting energy within the environment. Since this is a continual process, we are unaware of its occurrence, unless there is a significant alteration of the frequency or volume.

Because of our high metabolic rate, our constantly discharging nervous system, and our physical movement through surrounding force fields, we actually transform energy around us and in us. Free energy waves in space convert into waves with more specific forms as they pass through the varied densities of the body's tissues and energy fields. They mingle with our own subtle energy vibrations before they are discharged back into the external environment.

We can become aware of the variations in "lightning rod" currents as we move from one environment to another. For example, in walking through a grove of redwoods and walking through an apple orchard we experience energy in different ways. (See diagram.) The redwoods are tall and linear, have few low branches, and are sur-

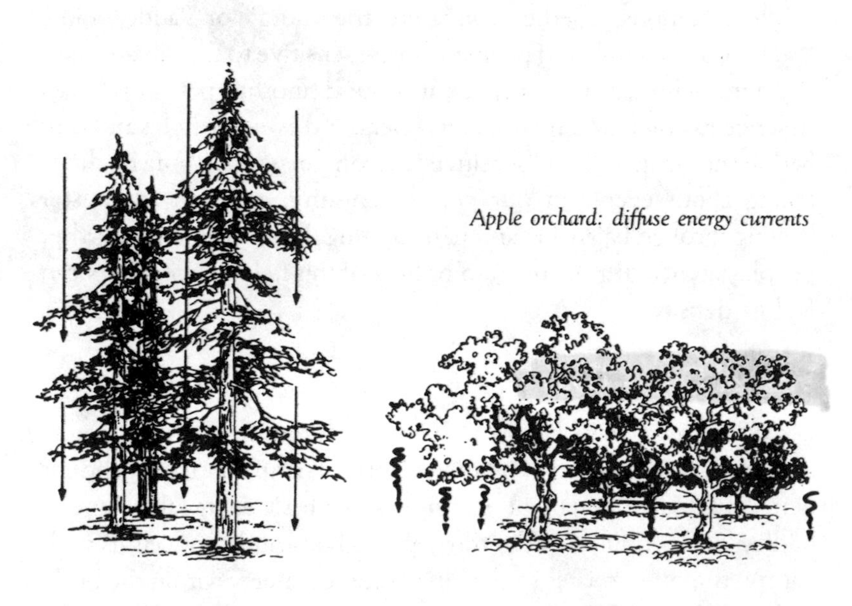

Apple orchard: diffuse energy currents

Redwood grove: streaming energy currents

rounded by little or no underbrush or scrub growth. In the orchard the trees are shorter, fuller, broader, and not as massive. The sensation felt in the redwood grove is quietness, with subtle sensations often described as streaming, humming, calming, or heavy. In an orchard the sensations we experience are less organized: random, rustling, lighter, softer, and diffuse. The exact experience will vary from person to person. Different physical forms of the antennae cause vibrations to vary as energy travels between the sky and the earth.

Throughout the world the ancients designated a number of areas as "power spots." They discovered certain places which had a special feeling and quality and, as the name implies, a particular power. A number of these power spots are located over underground streams and rivers; others are on hilltops, especially in areas surrounded by flat lands. Because of their locations these areas are strong natural antennae or interlocutors between the sky or air and the earth.

Church steeples act as strong conductors and produce greater force fields in the church. The high vaulted ceilings in large cathedrals amplify this effect, as one can experience by walking from the street into a large cathedral.

The body is an armature with different densities of tissue. The denser tissues conduct the stronger energy currents, and the densest part of our structure is the skeletal system. Consider a skeleton. Even after a person has died, the skeleton is holding an energy field. If it were not so, it would be dust. Energy is required to keep the molecules in the form of a skeleton, and the force fields of that individual are maintained within the bones. We can still gain insight into the individual who was once organized around that particular armature by feeling the tensions and torsions which remain in the skeleton.

Main Central Flow: The strongest currents conducted through us pass through the skull, backbone, pelvis, and legs, to be grounded to the earth at our feet. This is the portion of the skeletal system which is the most continually grounded, is the most vertical, and constitutes one major integrating flow connecting us to nature. In the Japanese energy therapy system known as *Jin Shin Juitsu* this spinal flow is called the main central flow or the Universal Life Flow.

Second Vertical Flow: A second vertical flow begins at the top of our shoulders and descends along the transverse processes of the vertebrae to the pelvis, where it joins the Universal Life Flow.

Third Vertical Flow: The third vertical flow branches through the shoulder girdle to the upper extremities, and is amplified by the use of our arms and hands.

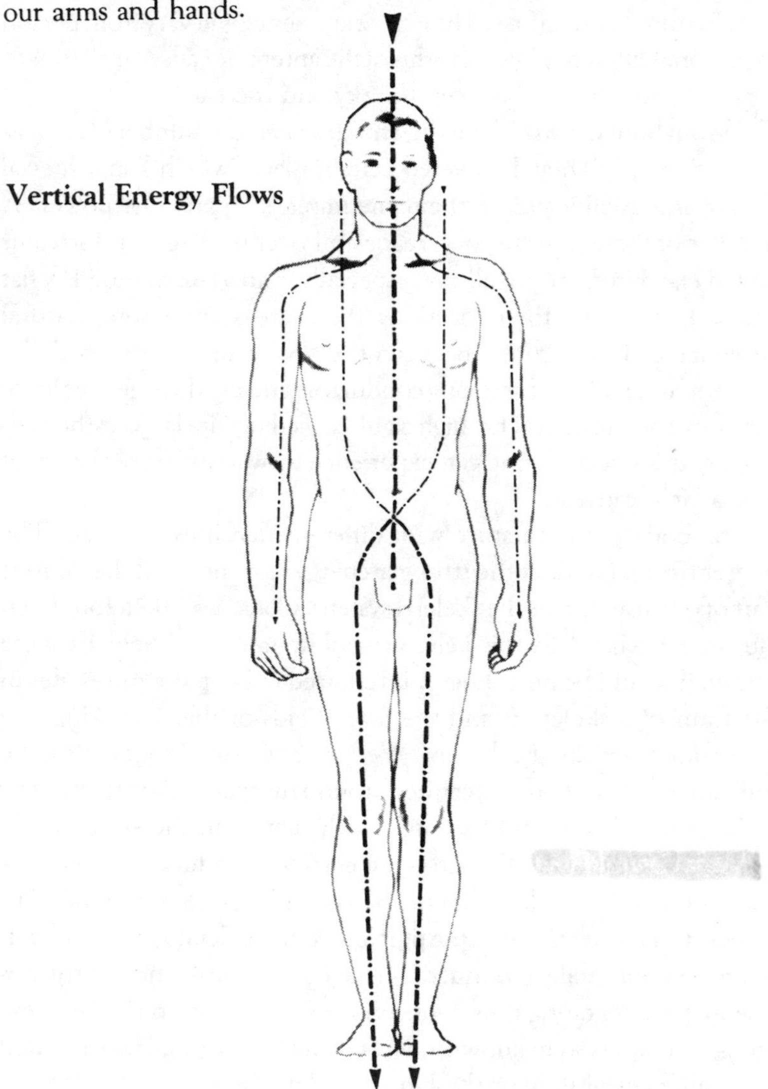
Vertical Energy Flows

Internal Energy Flows

Not only does energy exist as a background field, and as vertical flows through the body, but also as currents within the body, with identifiable paths and patterns. The energy that flows within us allows us to function as an individual unit. It is composed of three levels.

Internal Energy Flows — Deep Level: The currents within the deepest of these three levels flow through the bone and bone marrow and involve the skeletal system as a complete functioning unit. As we walk and move, the motion organizes the vibrations into a series of figure eight energy patterns around and through the body.

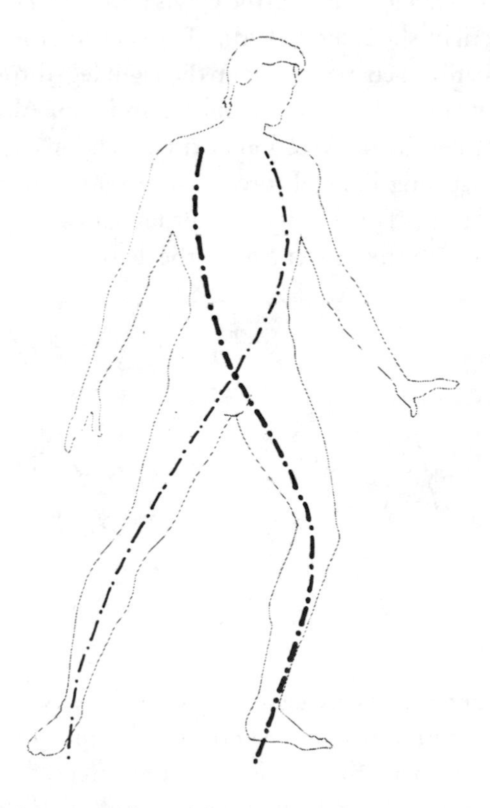

The deep energy flow of the internal energy system converts into a figure eight.

The body's theoretical center of gravity is located in the pelvis two inches in front of the second sacral segment. This is theoretical because the center is continually shifting as we walk and move in space.

The theoretical center of gravity of the body is located two inches in front of the second sacral segment.

Stepping on the left foot creates an energy vector which extends from the foot, up the left leg, through the pelvis and center of gravity of the body to the right shoulder and arm. Transferring the weight to the right foot creates an energy vector up the right leg, through the pelvis and center of gravity to the left shoulder and arm. Alternating from one foot to the other as we do in normal walking causes these two oblique intersecting lines of force to translate into a figure eight pattern in the body. This is further accentuated by swinging the arms in coordination with the movement of the legs.

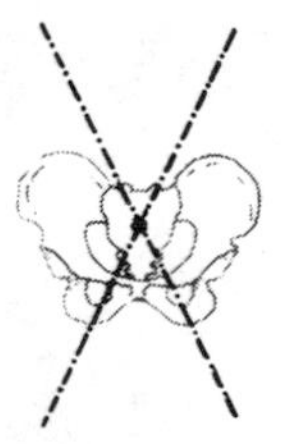

Oblique force fields created by walking

The concept of a "figure eight" is a two-dimensional oversimplification. The truth is that as the body weight shifts from one foot to another, yet another series of figure eights are created, this time on an oblique plane. Finally, as the body weight shifts from the heel to the toes of the weight-bearing foot, still another series of figure eights develops in the front-back plane. So in normal walking, the transference of weight from side to side, oblique to oblique and front to back, is balanced in the body around an ever-changing center of gravity within the pelvic bowl. Integrating the static figure eights into a three-dimensional model produces an hourglass shape.

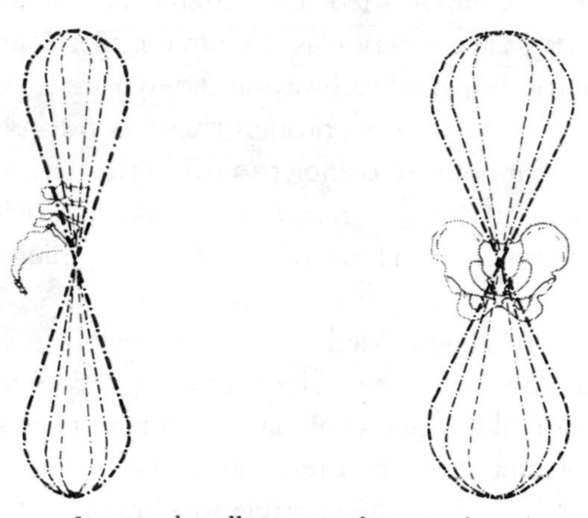

In normal walking an infinite number of figure eight patterns are created.

In the resting state, energy is believed to move in a constant pattern of flow up the left leg and out the right shoulder and arm; down the left arm and shoulder and out the right leg. The crossover at the center of gravity of the body continues.

Internal Flows—Middle Level: Soft tissues of the body, consisting of the muscles, nerves, blood, and the organs and viscera, house the middle layers of energy. This layer is the primary system in energy physiology; it "directs" or drives the energy body. It has a closer connection to the nutritional, mental, emotional, and spiritual needs of a person than does the deeper skeletal flow. Many cultures have developed detailed descriptions of this energy configuration.

One of the complete and detailed descriptions is found in acupuncture and Traditional Chinese Medicine. This is a complex, time-tested healing system based on centuries of clinical practice. A comprehensive presentation of acupuncture and its meridians and vessels is readily available and beyond the scope of this book, though some reference to its anatomy is important in our model.

In Traditional Chinese Medicine, energy is believed to move through pathways called meridians. The major meridians consist of twelve symmetrically paired pathways and two paired "vessels" (not blood vessels). Energy moves through these meridians constantly, taking twenty-four hours to complete a full cycle. The twelve meridians are classified as yin or yang, and each is associated with a specific body organ or function. They are grouped according to the five elements.

In Traditional Chinese Medicine the five elements are metal, water, wood, fire and earth. The elements represent the basic constituents or building blocks of nature, and each has a number of correspondents amplifying these relationships (see diagram). Beyond these specific correlations, the interrelationship of the five elements defines basic laws and principles of energy manifestation in our bodies and in nature. Among these are a creative or nurturing cycle (the Shen cycle) and a control or governing cycle (the Ko cycle). (See five elements chart.)

The "hidden anatomy" of energy in the body has been studied for thousands of years and has been described in detail in both ancient and modern acupuncture texts. The acupuncture points have been located along the meridians and vessels, and they are identified by palpating and observing the different "feeling" of an acupuncture point as compared to its surrounding tissue. With the advent of electrical measuring devices, points have been located on the body which have a low electrical resistance. These points coincide with the original acupuncture description. This documentation of the points gives further scientific credibility to the acupuncture model of energy anatomy.

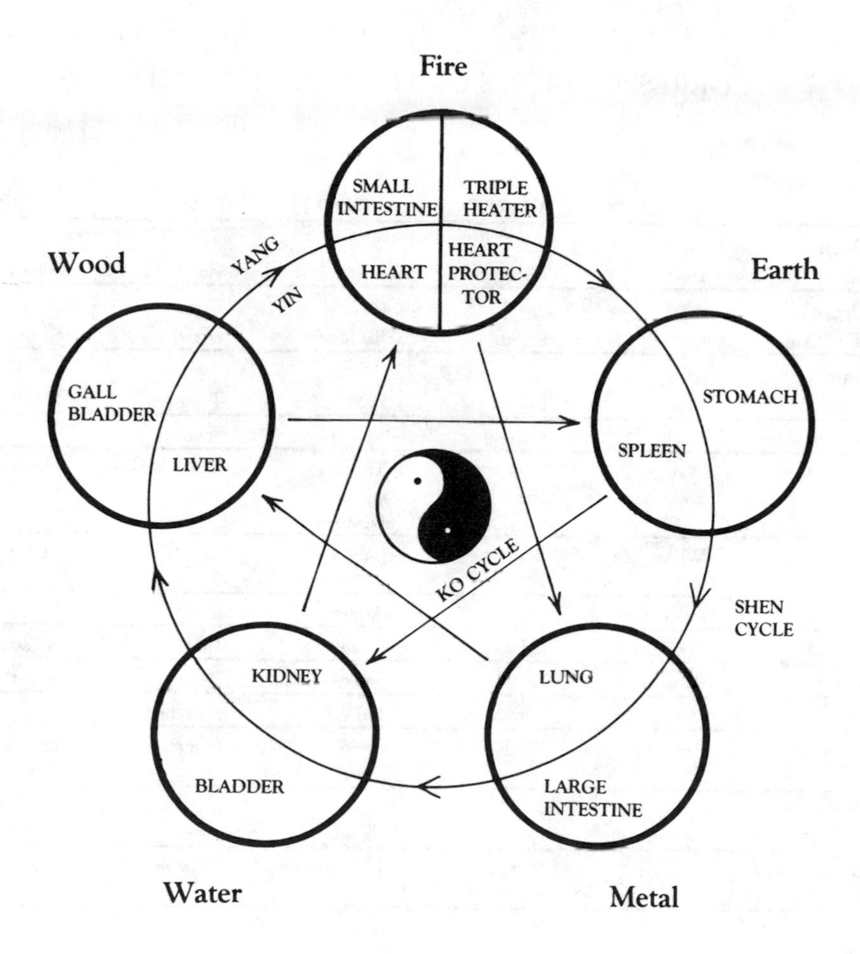

The Five Elements

Indicates the elements, the twelve main meridian pathways with their yin/yang association, and the two major energy cycles, the shen (creative) and the ko (control).

CORRESPONDENTS OF THE FIVE ELEMENTS

	METAL	WATER	WOOD	FIRE	EARTH
Organ (Zang/Yin)	Lung	Kidney	Liver	Heart	Spleen
Organ (Fu/Yang)	Colon	Bladder	Gall Bladder	Small Intestine	Stomach
Sense Organs	Nose	Ear	Eye	Tongue	Mouth
Sense	Smell	Hearing	Vision	Speech	Taste
Tissues	Skin Body Hair	Bone Head Hair	Tendon and Ligament	Blood Vessels	Muscles Flesh Lips
Color	White	Blue Black	Green	Red	Yellow
Emotion	Grief	Fear	Anger	Joy	Sympathy
Sound	Weep	Groan	Shout	Laugh	Singing
Taste	Pungent	Salty	Sour	Bitter	Sweet
Odor	Rotten	Putrid	Rancid	Scorched	Fragrant
Season	Autumn	Winter	Spring	Summer	Late Summer
Perverse Climates	Dryness	Cold	Wind	Heat	Dampness
Growth and Development	Reaping	Storing	Germination	Growth	Transfor-mation
Direction	West	North	East	South	Middle Center

Elemental Relationships

Nourishes	Water	Wood	Fire	Earth	Metal
Controls	Wood	Fire	Earth	Metal	Water
Controlled By	Fire	Earth	Metal	Water	Wood

The Meridians of Ch'i Energy: Anterior View

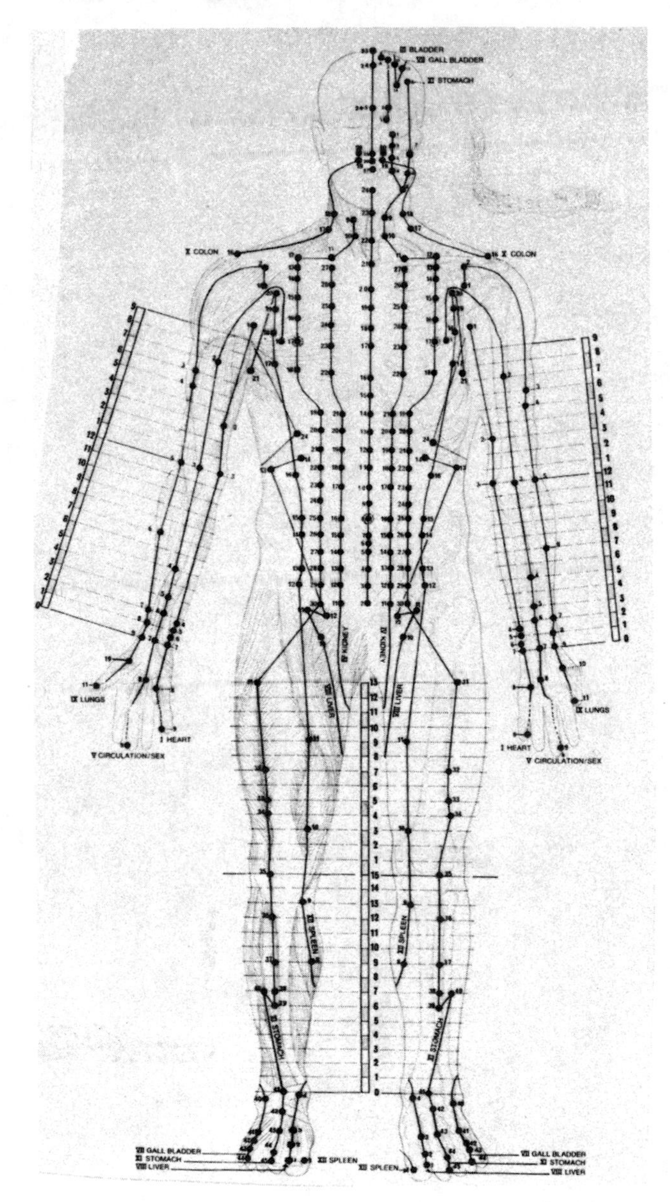

Courtesy of J. R. Worsley

The Meridians of Ch'i Energy: Posterior View

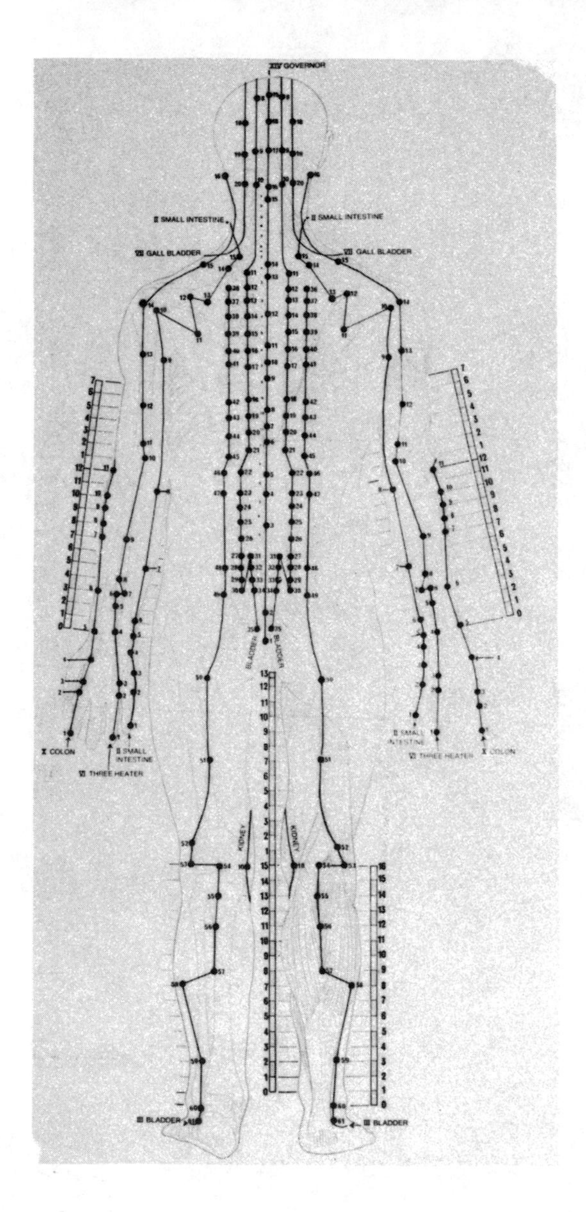

Courtesy of J. R. Worsley

The Meridians of Ch'i Energy: Lateral View

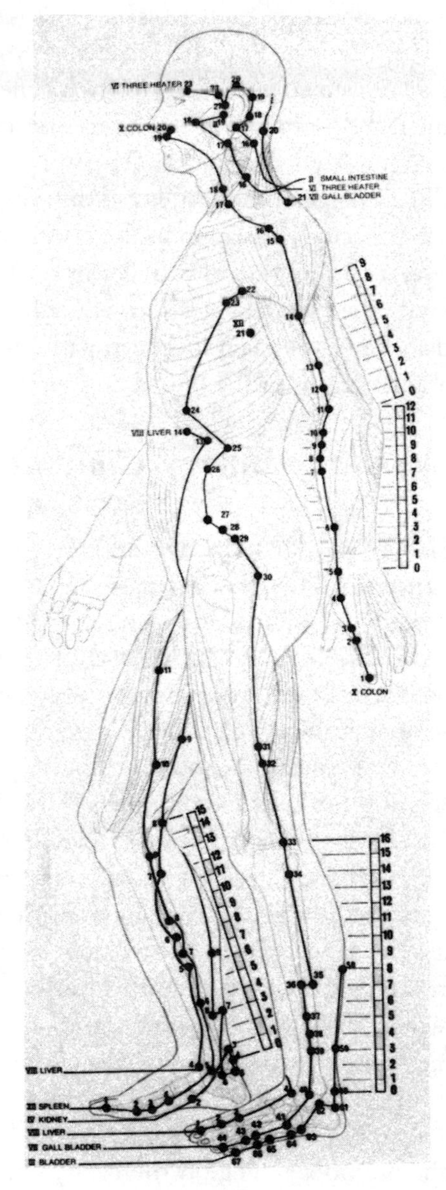

Courtesy of J. R. Worsley

Internal Flows — Superficial Level: Just as Traditional Chinese Medicine offers a clear and detailed anatomy of the middle layer of energy, so does it describe the superficial layer. This is the *wei chi*, a coarser, denser energy distributed in a nondifferentiated layer beneath the skin. It acts as an insulation, or protection, which buffers us from the outside environment and is our first line of defense against changes of climate, humidity, and external vibration. The wei chi controls the sweat glands and the energy in the tissues beneath the skin.

The wei chi has a specific circulation in the body which connects with the middle layer. If the wei chi is deficient or weak, perverse energy can penetrate the buffer layer and travel into the musculo-tendinous meridians, into the main meridian pathways, and, if not halted, to the internal organs of the body.

Ramifications of the Energy Conduit

Our high metabolic rate, our active nervous systems, and the ways we intersect our surrounding energy fields as we move, make us high-energy transformers. The volume of energy moving through us is generally greater than through upright objects of similar mass and weight. If a person is actually streaming energy (skilled public speaking, certain meditative or movement techniques, for example), the vertical currents conducted by the lightning rod function of the body create the form of funnels over the head and shoulders. This is similar to the funnels or whirlpools seen in water running rapidly through a drain.

The vertical currents have a cleansing effect on the internal energy system. As currents pass through us they intermingle with currents and vibrations already flowing in the body, and upon leaving our physical structures, represent composite mixtures of our inner and outer environments. This helps account for how the body of a meditator becomes so clear and organized, without direct attention to the physical body itself. Another ramification of this intermingling is that the exiting vibrations can be more harmonic or less harmonic than those which enter, depending on the clarity of one'.s internal

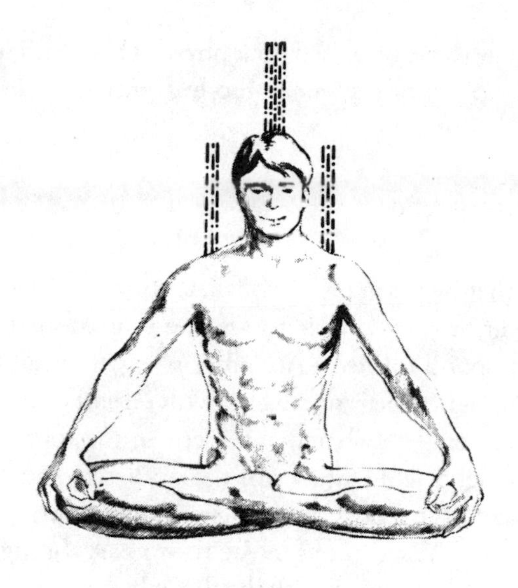

As a person streams energy the vertical currents convert to funnels or whirlpools.

state. People who have organized their physical body and subdued the "background noise" of the energy body transmit a clearer energy field.

Thought Transference

Thoughts themselves are vibrations. As they are emanating in the surrounding air, it is reasonable to assume that another person can receive and respond to them. A common experience of this intermingling energy is between an actively involved audience and a skilled teacher or lecturer. The vibrations present in the room contain the composite thoughts and attitudes of the audience and the speaker. When a speaker "turns on," the energy increases through his or her vertical flows. As the vibrations in the room pass through in greater number the speaker resonates with the thought waves of the audience and may begin to directly respond to the unspoken thoughts or questions of the audience. An interesting experiment in a small class is to concentrate on a question which is off the subject and see if the speaker addresses that particular issue. I have experienced this a number of times, and believe the speaker is reacting to my thoughts.

Energy in Human Communication

The vibrations of our auric fields affect our surroundings through the principle of resonance. We know that if we strike one tuning fork, and then place it among other tuning forks of the same or resonant pitch, those which have not been struck will begin to vibrate. It has also been observed that if a number of grandfather clocks are placed in a room, their pendulums, after a period of time, will swing synchronistically. On the human level, the menstrual cycles of women living together gradually become aligned.

As people come together their auric fields engage. There may be an instant sense of "connecting" or "bonding" as both persons' inner "tuning forks" of energy resonate at the same pitch. In some cases this happens only after several meetings. Resonance is facilitated if there is a shared experience or physical contact. The rituals of shaking hands, hugging, or making other salutory greetings are ways of lessening the tension and implementing resonance between the two fields. The word tension here is not meant in the usual sense of being in a state of tension or stress, but is used to suggest the tension between two forces, like notes struck on a musical instrument to make a chord, as they move toward synchronization or harmony.

Synchronization of energy fields is only one possibility. A person may contract his auric field, or increase its density to create a wall. Any manner of response is possible, depending on the situation between the two individuals.

I have found in teaching groups that if each session begins with a resonation circle (participants in a circle holding hands), the transmission and absorption of information is vastly enhanced. Friends of mine on a local school board have experimented with forming a resonating circle prior to each of their board meetings, and have found that the quality and quantity of their work significantly improved.

Communication is enhanced when the listener's field resonates to the speaker's words. The speaker then has a sense or experience of being "heard." We have all known the situation of talking with another person and feeling that we are not being heard — different from not being understood. It is as though what we were saying was either not engaging anything or hitting a blank wall, even when the hearer responds to the message. There is a feeling of completion when vibrations synchronize: a sense of separation when they are nonexistent or disharmonic. The best communication begins by energetically responding to another person.

As we become more open and resonate with other people's vibrations, however, our own clarity and centeredness become increasingly more important. If our own vibration is disorganized or off-center, it is more likely that we will synchronize with another person's *discord.*

Intentional Vibration Absorption

Some psychics consciously allow their auric field to simulate their client's, absorbing that vibration into their own internal energy system, and then describe the vibration they are experiencing. Another method used by psychics is to conduct the vibration through their vertical flows which allows them to "know" the client's situation without actually "experiencing" the vibration themselves.

Unintentional Vibration Absorption

I went through a period in my practice when I would walk into a room and without previous knowledge of the patient, begin to hurt in the same area of my body that the patient was hurting. While I found this a confirmation of my belief in resonance and vibration transference, it quickly became evident that this was not the way to conduct a busy medical practice.

Energy Buffers

There are a number of ways to minimize energetic resonance and absorption. The basic prerequisites for altering this dynamic are to recognize that we *are* responding to a vibration and then recognize that we can consciously buffer or dissociate from it. Knowing that energy follows thought, we can imagine our auric field changing density and becoming a durable insulator, protecting us from the other person's field. Brugh Joy, M.D., in his workshops, discusses creating an imaginary chrysalis around ourselves, just as a caterpiller constructs a cocoon during its transformation into a butterfly. We can create a chrysalis of energy by picturing ourselves surrounded by white light or a harmonic vibration of the exact density required to allow in any vibrations which are helpful, harmonic, or elevating while repelling vibrations which are disharmonic or detrimental. We can also intuitively gauge the density of the chrysalis to emit those vibrations we wish to send out and retain those we do not care to emit. With practice this procedure requires only a few moments, and performed each morning, it helps protect us from disharmony throughout the day.

At times stronger buffers are needed. We can envision a massive wall of energy in front of us. We can further contract our auric field by altering our behavior and becoming less emotive and emphatic, more detached and intellectual. If we have already begun to embody another person's pain or emotion, we can disconnect by promoting certain thoughts. Thinking of four or five obvious differences between us and the other person will usually suffice. Such thoughts as, "She's a woman, I'm a man"; "She's a brunette, I'm blond"; "He's not wearing glasses, I am"; or "He's wearing blue, I'm wearing green" are all effective. Any sort of distinction will promote energetic separation. By the time four or five distinctions are made, the unwanted resonance will be gone or significantly reduced.

Another way of decreasing vibratory absorption is to establish an *energetic interface* with the other person. In hands-on body work this can be done by paying attention to what we are literally feeling or perceiving at the point of bodily contact. Focusing thought on what is happening beneath our finger, elbow, or other point of contact with the other person, will automatically create an energetic interface.

Permanent Imprints of Energy on Objects

If we accept the existence of vibration and its movement, the idea of "empowering" objects or talismans has a more literal interpretation which exceeds the mental process of empowerment. As vibrations emanate from a person, they exist in the atmospheric environment and they can imprint on surrounding objects. The stronger and clearer the fields which are emitted, the more transference and imprinting there may be. It is even possible that artworks which are universally acclaimed as masterpieces were imprinted during their creation with the vibrations of the artist, and are still emitting fields to which the viewer is responding.

Summary of Energy Model

From modern science we learn that energy can exist as a particle or wave. In terms of the human body,the particle is manifest as physical and the wave as vibratory fields and currents. The sum total of all the vibration in the body composes the "energy body" or the "subtle body." The non-differentiated vibratory field pervades the physical body, is responsive to our thoughts and emotions, and extends beyond the body surface as a surrounding auric field. Like the currents moving through the ocean water, the non-differentiated vibration is organized into specific flows and configurations by forces within and outside the body, creating currents which both connect us to the whole of nature and enable us to function as an individual entity.

The currents which flow through us and integrate us with our external environment tend to be *vertical flows*, and they move according to the lightning rod principle. The densest of these currents move through the skeletal system.

Currents which move within us, and which are related to our functioning as an individual, are organized into three layers. The deepest layer flows through the skeletal system in the form of figure eights, or an hour glass, and is accentuated by walking and physical activity. The middle layer, flowing through the soft tissue, is described by Traditional Chinese Medicine. The pathways of energy in the middle layer tend to follow neurovascular bundles, muscle cleavages, and planes of fascial movement, and are augmented by soft tissue movement. Our physiological, mental, emotional, and spiritual functions are closely related and dependent on this middle layer of energy. The most superficial layer, the wei chi, is a layer of non-differentiated energy circulating just beneath the skin; it is affected by movement in the subcutaneous tissue, and serves a protective insulating function.

In the following chapter we will look at portions of this energy model (the main central vertical flow) from the viewpoint of the yoga philosophy. We will also see the interdependence of the particle and the wave as manifestations of the whole.

2

Bridges Between Eastern Yoga And Western Theories Of Anatomy

Discoveries in modern technology have led us to reexamine and seek new explanations in ancient energy concepts.

One day in a Zero Balancing Class as I was lecturing on skeletal anatomy and pointing out the normal curves of the spine, it suddenly occurred to me that, as the current of energy flows through the spine and around the spinal bends, as I believe it does, vortices of energy would be created at the major curves. As I studied the skeleton and imagined these vortices whirling, I recalled a picture of a meditating yogi with the overlay of the spinal chakras, and instinctively knew that the chakras must exist. They were not just abstract symbols of an ancient religious system; they actually corresponded to the structure of the human skeletal system and the laws of physics.

In the Eastern yoga philosophy, seven major energy centers, or chakras, are described along the spinal column. In Sanskrit, chakra literally means wheel, and they are described in ancient yoga texts as centers of energy in the body. Some yogis say these centers are only metaphors, depicting a map of a person's meditative experience; others, such as Gopi Krishna, believe they are actually associated with a person's individual evolution. Up to then I hadn't found evidence to support the actual existence of energy centers, but my insight at that moment settled the issue for me. This was further verified at a later time when I experienced heat and tingling in my spine during meditation and again when I learned to feel the energy fields with my hands.

I still recall the sense of relief I felt as this piece of the energy puzzle fell into place. The heretofore theoretical and abstract notions of the chakras became a reality for me as their form matched information I had learned in my study of Western medicine. These vortices of energy coincided with the curves of the skeleton. Not only did the centuries-old meditative insights of the yogis appear to be verified by the form of the physical body, but also from what I knew of the skeleton, and the behavior of energy in general, it seemed possible to make certain deductions about the relationships between the physical anatomy of the human body and the energetic nature of the chakras.

The Seven Major Spinal Chakras

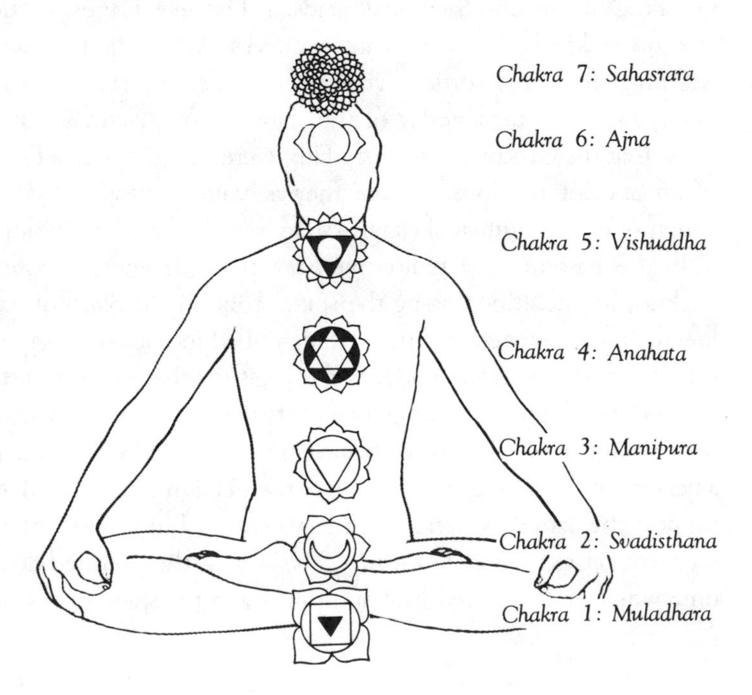

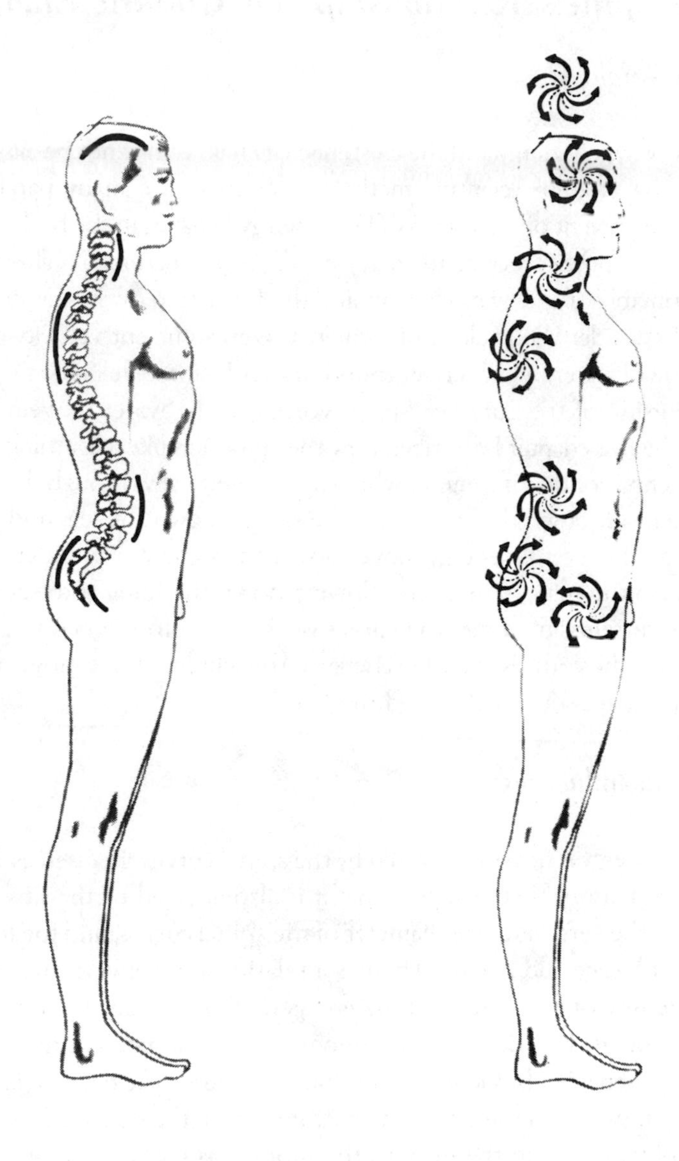

The vortices of chakral energy coincide with the curves of the skull and skeleton.

The Spine's Relationship To Chakra Energy

River Analogy

Pathways of energy and the existence of chakras may not be easy to prove by modern scientific methods, yet there are many parallels between ancient observations of how energy behaves in the body and the laws of physics relating to energy movement in nature. To illustrate the principle of energy movement and the formation of chakras in the body, consider the analogy of a river. Given sufficient velocity and volume of water, when a river rounds a bend a force field is set up at the outside of the curve causing a vortex in the water movement.

In the first chapter I described how the spine acts like a lightning rod or antenna conducting energy which moves vertically through the top of the head, down the spine, into the pelvis, down the legs and out through the feet. As energy moves down the spine it encounters the curves in the spine. The energy flowing down the spine corresponds to the currents in a river, the curves of the spine to the bend in the river, and the vortices of chakra energy to the whirlpool-like movement of the water as it flows around the bend.

Skeletal Influences

The energy is not only affected by the spinal curves themselves, but it seems reasonable to suppose that it is also affected by the size and mass of the vertebrae, the diameter of the spinal curves, and the form of the rib cage and pelvis. There is a relationship between the mass and density of an object and the energetic fields it can support. An object of greater density can support proportionately larger and denser energy fields. Generally speaking, the vertebrae become larger as they move from the top to the bottom. From the delicate first and second vertebrae in the neck to the more massive sacrum near the base of the spinal column, each of the spinal segments increases in size, excepting the four small bones which make up the coccyx, located beneath the sacrum.

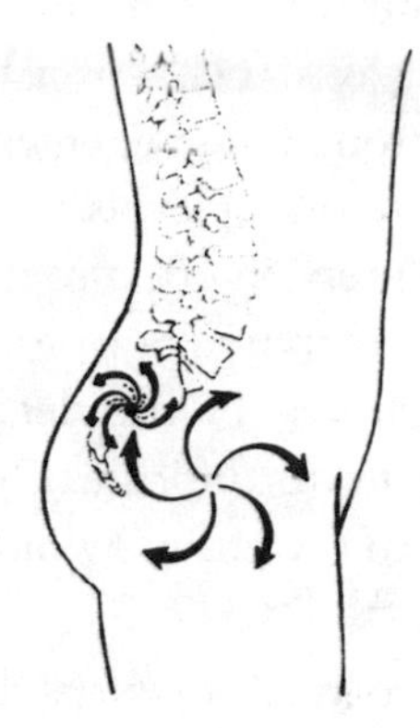

The first chakra diffuses, filling the pelvic bowl, and partially overlaps the second chakra.

The Coccyx and the First Chakra

When the energy currents reach the curve of the coccyx there is an abrupt decrease of the physical bone mass and the angle of its bend, resulting in the expansion of the energy vortex. The energy of the first chakra diffuses into a fine web-like field filling the pelvic bowl and partially overlapping the second chakra. This loosely-held energy of the first chakra then passes through the pelvis, legs, and down into the earth to complete the grounding of our body antenna.

The coccyx plays a critical role in allowing our energy fields to be grounded from the first chakra across the great distance from the pelvis to the earth. The reduction of bony mass and angle of curve at the coccyx acts as an energetic decompression valve allowing the energy vortex to spread out, become less dense, and be held less strongly. It can then more easily arc through the pelvis into the legs and ultimately into the earth.

Center of Body Gravity — The center of gravity in the body is a theoretical point in space located about two inches in front of the second sacral segment. The anatomic location is given in reference to the sacrum although energetically it closely corresponds to the center of the expanded first chakra. Because our center of gravity is so high from the ground, we have great mobility and movement potential. For the same reason we are inherently unstable, especially in stationary standing positions. The more strongly our energy is grounded into the earth the more stable we are on all levels. This grounding is facilitated by the energetic decompression effect of the delicate coccygeal bones. If the first chakra were anchored by a heavy bony mass the way the second chakra is anchored by the dense sacrum, overriding the force field would be more difficult. Our energetic connection across the great distance to the ground would be less secure and would lead to increased instability.

The energy expansion within the first chakra partially overlaps the densely-held second chakra. This phenomenon supports observations concerning the nature of the chakral system. Motoyama's text on *Theories of the Chakras* indicates there is a reciprocal flow of energy between the first and second chakras, and that it is not until the third chakra is activated that a constant upward movement of energies takes place. Each of the chakras affects its neighbors to some extent because as they expand they extend their perimeters and interlace. However, because of the specific skeletal relationships between coccygeal and sacral bone segments, we see the most dramatic overlapping of energy fields in the first and second chakras.

The Sacrum and the Second Chakra

The second chakra, in contrast to the first, is firmly anchored by the sacrum, the densest bone in the spinal column (the sacrum is actually formed by the fusion of five spinal segments into a single large mass). This anchor, plus the deep curve of the sacrum, functionally contributes to making the second chakra the densest of the spinal energy centers. The intensity and inherent force of this vortex is reflected in the power of sexuality. In kundalini yoga, the energy in this chakra is directed upwards in the spine, profoundly accentuating the activity of the centers lying above it.

The Lumbar Vertebrae and the Third Chakra

The third chakra is supported by the five heavy vertebrae that make up the lumbar curve. The middle of this curve is opposite the navel, and it is the navel, of course, that is our original source of energy during the prenatal period of our development. The third chakra is specifically related to our personal power and energy control.

Of the four weight-bearing curves of the spine, the lumbar and cervical curves, unlike the sacrum and thorax, have no additional bony support systems to help them carry their load. This "free standing" quality of these spinal segments relates to the personal initiative associated with the chakras of the lumbar (third chakra) and cervical (fifth chakra) areas: namely, "personal power" and "personal creativity" respectively.

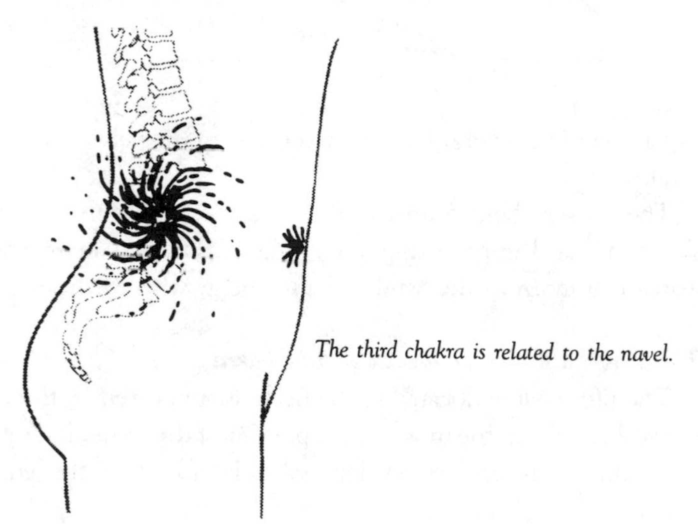

The third chakra is related to the navel.

The Thoracic Vertebrae and the Fourth Chakra

The fourth energy center, the heart chakra, is located in the chest, and is associated with the long thoracic curve of the spine. This long curve allows the energy field to spread out more than it does in the second and third chakras. The expansive nature of this area is further encouraged by the "pull" of the bony structure of the rib cage ; a similar

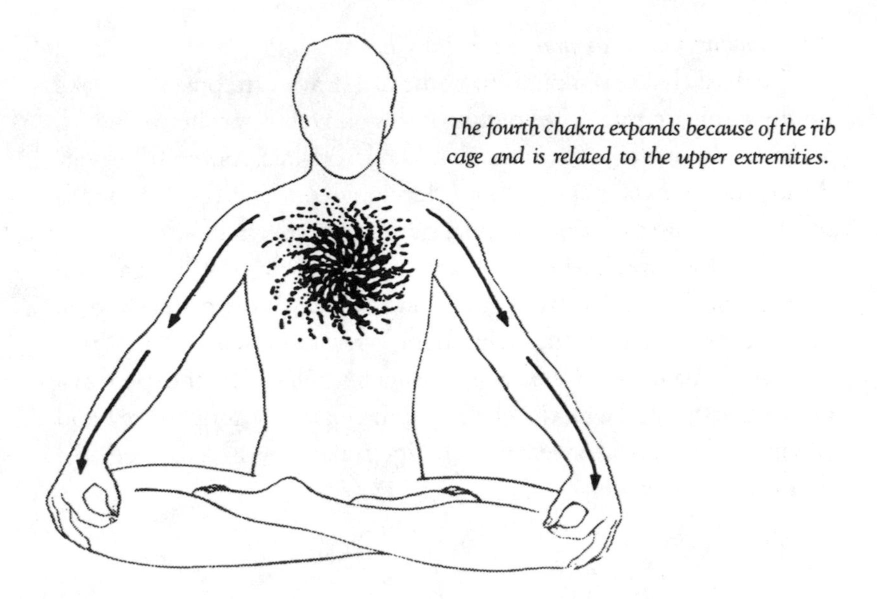

The fourth chakra expands because of the rib cage and is related to the upper extremities.

expansion of the energy is found in the area of the pelvic bowl and the skull.

The loosely held fourth chakra is associated with the scapula, shoulders, and upper extremities. This is reflected in several yoga asanas that integrate the hand and arm energy with the heart chakra.

The Cervical Vertebrae and the Fifth Chakra

The fifth chakra, located in the neck, is supported by the delicate cervical vertebrae, the most mobile portion of the spine. It is related to communication, and as we have already noted, is the chakra of personal creativity.

The Brow and the Sixth Chakra

The sixth chakra, known as the "third eye," is related to the forehead and is associated with intuition. The bowl configuration of the skull encourages the expansion of this center. Some yogis working with this chakra focus their awareness at the back of the skull and "look through" the chakra and through the forehead from the inside out, much as we "look through" our normal eyes from inside our heads.

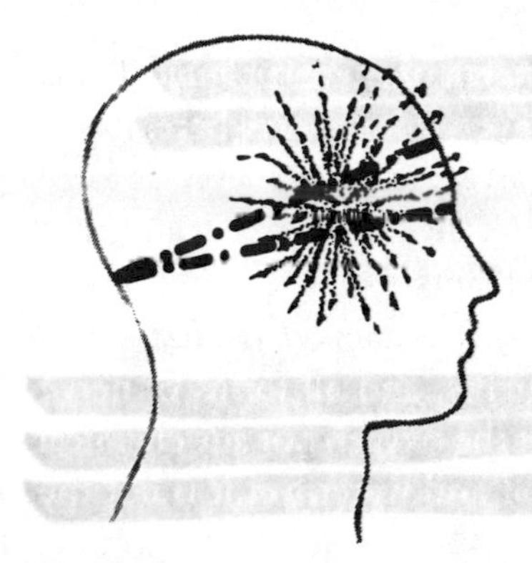

Some yogis focus awareness from the back of the skull, through the sixth chakra, to the back of the forehead.

The Top of the Skull and the Seventh Chakra

The seventh chakra is associated with the top of the skull, where energy currents from the Universal Life Flow first make contact with the body.

Chakra Energy Bridging Physical And Spiritual Worlds

In the Hindu system, the theory of chakras is related to the Eastern belief in a Universal Soul with which the individual's soul can unite. This unification can happen if a person is able to conquer or transcend *Maya*, the state of illusion and duality which, according to yoga, most of us recognize as our everyday reality: a world of phenomena bound by space and time. In yoga, one can develop a state of consciousness where there is the experience of nonduality and where time and space seem to merge. One transcends subject and object, and "knower, knowledge, and the known" fuse into one.

There are many different paths in the yogic system, but common to all are the basic tenets of developing purity of the physical and mental body, learning concentration of thought and breath control, and quieting the mind to experience the pure consciousness that lies within each one of us.

Prana

Central to all yogic thought is the concept of energy or *prana*. Prana is the universal energy which suffuses everything everywhere. It is *in* all forms of matter, and yet it is not matter; it is the energy or force which animates matter. It is, for example, the life force that animates the material bodies of all animals and plants. Prana is manifest in a variety of forms that scientists often classify as energy manifestations: gravity, electricity, body actions, thoughts, and all forms of nerve currents. Prana is in the air, but it is not the oxygen nor any chemical constituent of it. It resides within food and water, yet it is not the calories or fluid.

An individual can learn to influence this force in a number of ways. One way is called *pranayama*, which deals with breath control. Other ways include the use of *asana* or body postures, mental concentration, meditation, introspection, chanting, visualization, and fasting.

As the yogi learns more about the nature of prana and the ability to sense it in his or her own body, many possibilities arise. Prana can be stored or released from the body, can be transmitted from one person to another, and can be transmitted over great distances. A number of yogis have been studied by the Western scientific community: these yogis have demonstrated the ability to control autonomic functions of the body including heart rate, blood pressure, intestinal movement, pain control, and the rate of tissue healing.[1]

Siddhis

Paranormal abilities such as clairvoyance, psychokinesis, and telepathy known as *siddhis* are common "by-products" of the development of prana control and activation of the spinal chakras. Yogi aspirants are cautioned not to be sidetracked by siddhi powers. The purpose of yoga is not to develop any special abilities but rather to

[1] Rama Swami, *Voluntary Control Project.* Research Department, Menninger Foundation, Topeka, Kansas.

develop a state of internal control where one can rise above the world of phenomenality and duality into that of union with the Universal Soul.

The Yoga View of the Human Body

Yogis describe the human body as composed of three different manifestations or divisions, not dissimilar from the body-mind-spirit triad common in our Western culture. These three divisions or "bodies" are the physical, mental or "subtle," and the spiritual or "causal" body. Using a different vocabulary, the life force is divided into three parts, consisting of inert matter (physical), energy movement (emotional-mental), and the intelligence of nature (causal).

Physical Body — According to this line of thought, the physical body itself is without vitality or spirit and is composed of flesh, blood and bone.

Subtle Body — The subtle body contains the vital spirit or life force. In and of itself the vital spirit has no form, since its shape and movement are defined by the form and activity of the physical body. The subtle body is less stable than the dense physical form, and it adjusts rapidly to shifts in a person's physical, mental, or emotional state. It is responsive to changes in the external environment, such as the time of day, the seasons of the year, the phases of the moon, and the changes in the immediate temperature and barometric pressure. Changes in the subtle body directly affect the physical body, though in a slow fashion, due to the greater density of the latter.

Causal Body — The third body, the causal or spiritual body, encompasses the intelligence of nature, universal wisdom, direct knowing, and it is this force that connects us to the universe outside ourselves.

Nadis

In the yogi model, energy travels within the subtle body through thousands of channels of varying size known as *nadis*. These nadis are interconnected energy channels which weave throughout the body like webs. They originate at the navel, and many follow the blood vessels and nerves of the physical body.

At birth, with the severance of the umbilical cord, a fundamental and dramatic shift occurs in the body as the source of prenatal life is cut. We suddenly must get oxygen from the breath, nutrition from food, and prana from both. Following parturition, the navel continues to function as an energetic center of great power, having been the originating point of the nadis.

Sushumna — Of the many nadis in the body, the three most important ones are the *sushumna*, the *ida*, and the *pingala*. All arise from the base of the spine in the area of the coccyx and perineum. The sushumna is the astral tube which runs through the spinal column itself. Originally the lower end of the sushumna is closed, and at its base resides great potential energy. The yogis describe this untapped energy as held in a coiled form of three and a half turns, known as *Kundalini* (coiled) or serpent power.

Ida and Pingala — The ida and pingala run up either side of the spine, the ida beginning on the left and the pingala on the right. The prana carried in the ida is described as being of a cooling nature, inhibiting or slowing body organ functions, and associated with mental and psychic activities. It is considered a "lunar" energy. The pingala is nearly the opposite of ida. It carries heat, stimulates the organs of the body, controls the prana and visceral activities, and is fiery in nature. It is associated with the sun.

Both of these nadis begin at the base of the spine and ascend, passing through the nostrils and ending on the forehead at a point between the eyebrows. Some yogic texts indicate the ida and pingala rise parallel along either side of the spine to their termination; others describe these two nadis as interweaving across the spine and ending in the forehead.

There is a correlation between the Western medical concept of "the law of the flexible rod," and the ida and pingala energy currents. According to the principle of the flexible rod, whenever an object is bent across a curve an element of rotation occurs along the axis; and when a rotation is introduced across a curve, there is an element of side

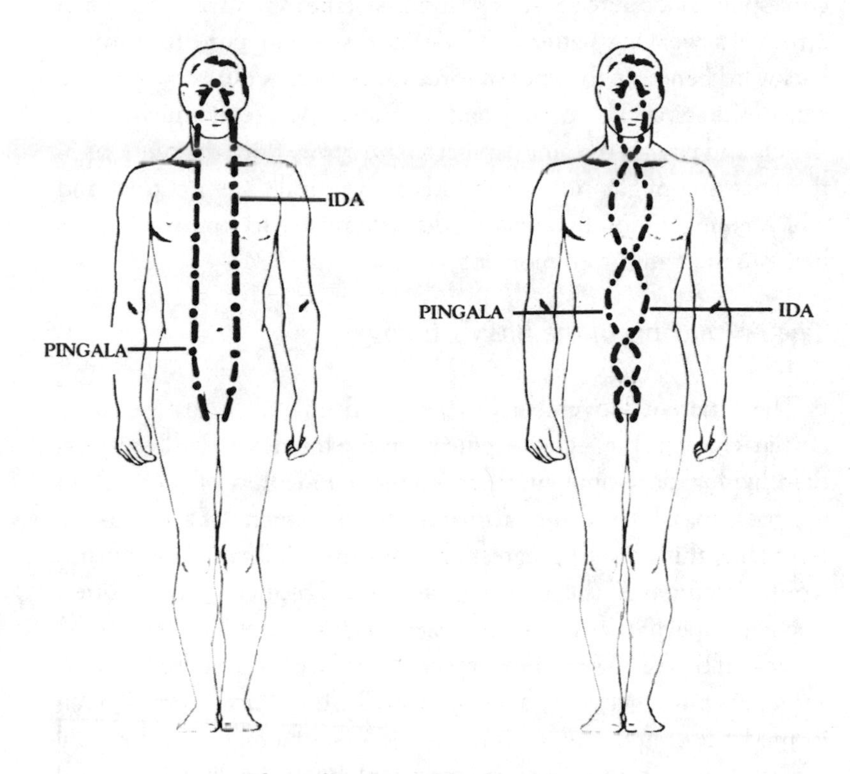

The configurations of the ida and the pingala nadis are influenced by body motion.

bending. Thus in the body, because of the natural spinal curves, whenever we make a side bending motion it puts a rotary torque into the spine. When we rotate the spine, it activates a side bending motion. In forward or backward bending, however, we do not bend *across* curves, nor do we have any rotation of the spine. These motions are "pure" movements in one plane only.

According to physical principles, the continuing interrelationship of side bending and rotation, which is common in every step we take and most motions we make, will generate two lines of energy moving up either side of the spine, which will crisscross over the spine. This corresponds closely to those descriptions of the ida and pingala, which indicate a weaving pattern. While at rest or in pure forward or backward bending, the lines of force do not cross but run along the side of the spine. This corresponds to those yogic texts which depict the ida and pingala running parallel to the spine. Both descriptions of the energy configurations of the ida and pingala seem correct and which configuration these two nadis take relates to how the body is being used at any given moment.

The Awakening of the Body's Energy

The inherent movement in the spinal chakras is generated by currents moving through the spine from the top down. In the process of individual development, there is a retrograde flow of energy from the base up, which further activates the movement of the chakras. Normally, this upward progression from first chakra to the seventh would occur over the person's lifetime. Through the centuries, however, specific activities have been discovered which hasten the process of this retrograde movement, stimulate these energy centers, and accelerate a person's "development." These "discoveries" often formed the framework of the "secret" teachings of the mystical schools, white and black magic, internal alchemy, healing rituals, and developing paranormal abilities.

In the yoga philosophy, "the awakening of the kundalini" and the opening of the sushumna nadi is the initiation of the accelerated awakening process. There is *shakti* (energy) stored in the pelvis at the base of the spine, the kundalini, described and often experienced as a "serpent" coiled in three and a half turns. When this stored energy is activated and the serpent is aroused, it penetrates the sushumna pathway; the shakti moves upward in the spinal column and activates the major centers of the spine, the chakras. Much time and effort on the yogi's part are required for raising the energy to penetrate a chakra. When the kundalini energy does enter a chakra the increased vitality causes the wheel of the chakra to spin faster, expanding the vortex of energy farther out from the center of the chakra, stimulating and enhancing any and all functions — physiological, psychological, spiritual — associated with that center. These vibrations spread throughout the body. The effects of the awakened kundalini, therefore, are not confined to the spinal energy centers only, but become manifest throughout one's entire being.

The kundalini may be aroused in a number of ways. It can happen spontaneously. It can be activated through the touch or influence of a teacher or guru (through *shaktipat* or spiritual awakening); it can be activated through internal practices such as meditation, concentration, and visualization.

One specific meditation technique is to blend or unite the polar forces of ida and pingala. The currents of ida and pingala are balanced force fields along either side of the spine and are associated with the polarity or duality orientations within the body/mind. To the extent that they can be forged into one current at the base of the spine, the kundalini energy will be activated and the sushumna pathway opened. The energy will start to move upward in this central channel as a single current and there will begin a fundamental shift in the orientation of the yogi. The experiences and awareness of duality will diminish and those of unity or oneness will become prevalent. Once the sushumna pathway is fully opened through all the seven major chakras the experience of the yogi is described as transcending the phenomenal world of duality, the limitations of time and space, and of merging in oneness with the Universal Soul.

The Chakra Model

The implications of the energy model I presented in chapter one expand enormously as we realize that the main vertical flows of current through the spine that orient us to nature are directly related to the ancient yoga model of chakra energy. In this model the chakras have a number of correspondents, just as the five elements do in the Chinese system. Each energy center has a physical location in the body and is associated with a nerve plexus, endocrine gland, and physiological and emotional attributes. Each has a particular color, sound, and geometric form. Beyond these specifics are elaborate pictorial and mythologic associations which have developed over the centuries. These poetic statements and myths share the visions and experiences yogis have encountered as they have activated the specific chakras.

An examination of each chakra will suggest ways that knowledge of the yoga system might apply to our working energy model. What follows is a brief description of the chakras according to their evolutionary function.

The First Chakra

The first of the seven major chakras is the "root" or "base" chakra. Its physical location is at the base of the spine in the perineum (the area between the anus and genitals), and is associated with the coccygeal and sacral nerve plexus. Our basic foundations and personal sense of security, self-esteem, and self-worth reside here. Its functions are connected with personal survival needs and skills: eating, sleeping, the "fight or flight" syndrome, and relating with the material world. Within this chakra lies the dormant creative energy of the coiled serpent, the kundalini.

In *The Mythic Image*, Joseph Campbell says:

> One may think of the kundalini on this level as compared to a dragon; for dragons, we are told by those who know, have a propensity to hoard and guard things; and their favorite things to hoard and guard are jewels and beautiful young girls. They are unable to make use of either, but just hang on, and so the values of their treasury are unrealized, lost to themselves and to the world. On this level, the serpent queen kundalini is held captive by her own dragon-lethargy. She neither knows nor can communicate to the life that she controls any joy; yet will not relax her hold and let go. Her key model is a stubborn *here I am and here I stay.* The first task of a yogi then must be to break at this level the cold dragon grip of his own spiritual lethargy and release the jewel maid, his own shakti (energy) for ascent to those higher spheres where she will become his spiritual teacher and guide to the bliss of immortal life beyond sleep.

The Second Chakra

The second chakra is associated with the sacrum, and the translation of its Sanskrit name means, "her special abode," or "one's special abode." This chakra is associated with the kidneys, gonads, and sexuality, and is connected to the sacral and prostatic nerve plexus. In this area resides stored ancestral energy and a portion of the collective unconscious. When a person's focus resides in this chakra, everything is flavored by sensuality and sexuality, and events are interpreted from that viewpoint. The very dense force fields of this center act as a block for the rising of the kundalini energy through and beyond this chakra.

Inherent in the Hindu philosophy is the notion that energy which is generated and activated through the sexual chakra may be brought upwards along the sushumna to higher levels of the person's awareness and can be used as a creative force in their internal growth. A portion of the second chakral energy is used for procreation, but its great potential is to activate higher centers within the sushumna path.

In religious orders throughout the world, both Eastern and Western, the role of sexuality or perhaps more accurately, the power of this second chakra, is specifically addressed. At one extreme are the monastic, chaste religious paths which advocate holding the full sexual powers inside the body for transmutation to higher powers. The opposite extreme is the Tantric school of yoga which prescribes overt sexuality, and instructs the aspirants in ways to achieve "unity" and "oneness" through energy inherent in the sex act. In both of these extremes the power of the second chakra is being harnessed in hopes of advancing the individual along the spiritual path, toward the point of unity and a closer, deeper relationship to the Universal Soul.

The Third Chakra

The third chakra is the "jewelled lotus" or "city of the shining jewel." Located near the solar plexus, behind the navel, it is a center of digestive fire, from which vital energies are distributed. This is the center for personal power. In prenatal development our source of energy was through the umbilical cord, hence the significance of the location of this chakra. When a person is motivated primarily from the third chakra, competition, conquest, and control of situations are of paramount importance.

Sexuality, when acted on from this chakra, has more to do with conquest, revenge, and control than with procreation or the erotic sensuality of the second chakra.

The Fourth Chakra

The fourth chakra embodies the heart, is related to the thymus gland and is the first nonduality-oriented chakra which the rising energy encounters. It represents a major transition and shift of orientation from the first three chakras. Its Sanskrit name means "not stuck," unbeaten or unbroken. The chakra deals with the principle of unity, and here for the first time we see the issue of free will. The three lower chakras are concerned with aspects of cause and effect, but in this nondual chakra we move away from this dynamic into one of action rather than reaction.

Here in the fourth chakra we find compassion, a sense of belonging, unity, and unconditional love. Compassion is more accessible when there is freedom from competition and duality and there is a sense of fullness and personal fulfillment. The emotion of the heart is joy and laughter, a counterpart of fullness and overflowing. The heart chakra is connected to our sense of touch and the power of psychokinesis.

According to Campbell, the heart "is a place where sound is heard that is not made by any two things striking together. The only sound which is not made by two objects striking is that of the creative energy of the universe, the hum, which is antecedent to things and of which things are precipitations."

When the kundalini energy breaks the barrier between the third and fourth chakra, a major transformation takes place within the individual. With the experiencing and "knowing" of unity comes a fundamental shift to feeling one's self truly a part of the universe and of nature. Feelings of alienation and duality begin to drop away. We harmonize with society and the ecologic systems around us, and think in terms of "we" and "us" rather than dealing with the external world as separate and distinct from ourselves.

The Fifth Chakra

The fifth chakra pertains to the throat and thyroid gland, and the Sanskrit translation is "purified." It is related to nurturance and personal creativity. In the heart center reside compassion and unconditional love, both implicated with giving or being with another. In the throat chakra resides the ability to receive, to admit in, to be truly cared for. In the esoteric sense, this is to receive "grace" and wisdom, and to gain access to an inner, unlimited source. This chakra is connected with artistic endeavor, articulation, teaching, writing, and the creative expression of our "true" inner self. It has a special relationship to the second chakra in terms of creation: personal creation and creation of the species. In order to receive and be nurtured as well as be creative and expressive, the yogi strives to clear his mind of secondary things to experience the unveiled voice and light of Brahma (God). This pure experience leads to the siddhi powers of clairaudience, and the ability to endure long deprivations of food or drink.

The Sixth Chakra

The sixth chakra, the ajna, resides within the skull. Its body surface location is between the eyebrows on the forehead. It is associated with the pineal gland. The Sanskrit translation of ajna means "command." In the Western world it is referred to as the "third eye." This is the seat of intuitive knowledge and the paranormal attributes of telepathic communication and clairvoyant perception. According to *Yoga and Psychotherapy*,[2] "opening the third eye means integrating the right

2 Swani, Rama, Rudolph Ballantine, M.D., Swami Ajaya, Ph.D., *Yoya and Psychotherapy: The Evolution of Consciousness* (Himalayan Institute of Yoga Science and Philosophy: Pennsylvania, 1976), p. 226.

and left sides (of the brain). It means bringing together judgment and discrimination, which characterize the left side, with the openness and . . . the intuitive world that characterize the right. It means bringing together these two partial, inaccurate ways of knowledge into an integrated whole." In the yoga cosmology, the ajna is where the ida and pingala meet and join the sushumna to form the single energy channel which continues up to the seventh chakra at the top of the head.

There is a direct connection between the first and the sixth chakra via the ida and pingala. During chakral meditations, if attention is first given to the brow chakra before stimulating the lower centers, the released energy has a direction of flow which encourages a more effective energetic meditation.

In the esoteric tradition, opening the sixth chakra leads to a form of *samadhi*, a high meditative state, which is beyond time, space, and causality. Although this state cannot be adequately described, it is associated with a sense of perfect well being, of being at one with the universe, without judgment, perfectly in tune with the present moment. Beyond this, Ramakrishna states:

> Whenever I try to describe what kind of vision I experience. . . and think what kind of vision I am witnessing, the mind rushes immediately up, and speaking becomes impossible. (The aspirant) then has direct knowledge of the supreme Self . . . there is only a screen transparent like glass. The supreme Self is so near that it seems as if one is merged in (It), identified with (It). But identification is yet to be.[3]

The Seventh Chakra

The seventh center is the sahasrara, the "thousand-petalled lotus," the crown chakra. It is associated with the pituitary gland, the master endocrine gland in the body. Energy moving up the channel from the brow chakra reaches the Brahmin point, where part of the forces

[3] Rama, Ballantine, Ajaya, *Yoga and Psychotherapy*, 269.

flow into the chakra, while the rest are reflected back into the physical, subtle, and causal bodies of the individual.

In the kundalini progression, the highest state of consciousness resides in the thousand-petalled lotus. The boundaries between I and thou disappear, and seer and seen are merged into one. This is the true samadhi.

Body Purification and Kriyas

In ancient times, according to tradition, an aspiring yogi would sit for months or years at the feet of his guru before receiving the spark of energy (shaktipat) which would awaken the kundalini and ignite the ascending energy. This lengthy apprenticeship was to allow for the purification of the aspirant's internal vibration, so that when the energy surged upward through the body it would not lead to injury, illness, or psychosis. It is repeatedly stated in yogic literature that the kundalini process is not without real dangers, and one should not embark on this path without the guidance of an experienced teacher.

In the process of activating powerful subtle energies which move through body, mind, and emotions, body obstructions and densities are encountered. A common phenomenon with people on the path of kundalini is the *kriya.* A kriya is an involuntary response caused by resistance to the passage of energy through a dense or congested area of the body. Kriyas may be of a major or minor nature; may be temporary, ongoing, or recurrent; may involve any level of the body, mind, and spirit. Common forms of physical kriyas are involuntary jerkings or twitchings of the body, chattering of the teeth, flickering of the eyelids, or spasmodic movement of some portion of the body.

The first time I encountered a major physical kriya was at a meditative retreat. A man was on the ground, appearing to my medically trained eye to be suffering an epileptic seizure. I rushed over, intending to give first aid, when an experienced meditator came up and calmly touched him on the leg. In a brief moment the seizure began to subside, and the man returned to normal consciousness. To my further surprise, I found, talking with him later, that his experience was not only not a frightening one, but fulfilling and enriching, and was followed by a great sense of peace and serenity. Again my medical model was shaken, and I have wondered since how many kriya experiences have been diagnosed and treated as "epilepsy."

Kriyas may also be expressed in forms such as breath patterns (spontaneous pranayama), sounds (nada), or beautiful hand movements and dance forms (mudras). It has been suggested that the asanas of hatha yoga were actually derived from special mudra kriyas, which people spontaneously assumed in deep states of meditation. Voluntarily reduplicating these positions can help open specific centers and lead back to a meditative experience.

Kriyas may take the form of sudden outbursts of emotion, spontaneous crying, periods of sadness and depression, or buzzing and tingling throughout the body. They may manifest as "speaking in tongues," or "automatic writing." Any manner of behavior is possible depending on the power of the kundalini energy and the nature of the resistance encountered. In extreme cases, especially where trained teachers were not available, destructive behavior or psychosis have occurred.

The vast majority of kriyas should not be feared. With continuing yoga, meditation, and purification, the obstructions within the body lessen, and the tendency to have kriyas ceases.

Chakral Energy and Human Development Theory

The normal, unstimulated awakening or energizing of the chakras follows a natural progression in one's human growth and development, often considered in seven-year cycles. The first chakra deals with self-esteem and survival skills. Moving into adolescence the second, that is, sexual chakra, is energized, In late adolescence, as the third chakra gains energy, there is an increasing sense of self-awareness, of growing personal power, feelings of being able to conquer the world. As the third chakra is more fully felt, power of possession, control, and competitiveness play a large role.

With the introduction of relationships in our lives, of marriage and the birth of children, the need to be concerned for others beyond ourselves begins a natural impetus toward compassion and unconditional love, as seen in the fourth chakra. Over time, with increasing life experiences and maturity, comes wisdom, and we take on the role of "teacher," moving into high energy in the fifth chakra with internal inspiration and intellectual creativity. As one approaches older age, religious acts of life are naturally more relevant, with contemplation of death (and possible rebirth) leading us toward high activity in the sixth and ultimately the seventh chakras.

This is the inherent order of the progression, although all the chakras are acting and overlapping each other all the time. The functions of each of these energy centers are with us throughout our lives, although each one prevails or "leads the dance" at different times depending on where a person is in his or her developmental sequence and life process.

Windows of Perception

Energetically the path through life may be seen as a spiral, where we perceive life issues from the different windows of perception of the seven energy centers. In adolescence, for instance, when sexual energy is forcefully emerging, we see the universal issue of each of the chakras — survival, sexuality, personal power, compassion, wisdom, and insight — through the "window" of the second chakra. We interpret our personal history and our relationship with our parents, family, and friends through this portal. The same issues, the same questions, come up in each period of our lives as we spiral upward, but have different implications as our vantage points change. How frequently have we found ourselves dealing with issues that we thought we had solved many years earlier?

Visualization

Through the power of visualization we can consciously access any chakral window and influence our own behavior. For example, anger (third chakra) is one of the basic emotions. If we are involved with this emotion, there are a number of options for dealing with it. We can express it directly. We can shift the energy (sublimate it) into an alternative action. We can suppress it or "bottle up" the energy, although there is general agreement that to habitually deal with anger in this way is ultimately unhealthy. We can deliberately choose to "move" the vibration from the third to another chakra and allow it to be expended in that mode. In this instance, for example, I have frequently visualized the energy moving from my third chakra to the fourth, and have allowed the vibration of anger or frustration to dissipate through compassion and understanding.

In a recent workshop, couples were seated a foot apart facing each other and asked to "connect" their respective chakral energies through visualization. As part of the exercise they were to pay attention as to how it felt when the centers actually connected, to assess the completeness of each contact, and be conscious of the feeling of being in connection with another person. The couples then were instructed to disconnect, paying attention to the process of reestablishing their individual energy fields.

In sharing the experience, most everyone had "a sensation" when the centers connected, and some awareness of the degree of their connectedness. Everyone experienced a feeling of being connected to the other person. Interestingly, one couple, who had been having undefined stress in their relations for a number of months, connected all centers well with the exception of the third chakra. Out of the difficulty they had in making this bridge came new insights as to the nature of their problem, and they began to see ways to resolve it.

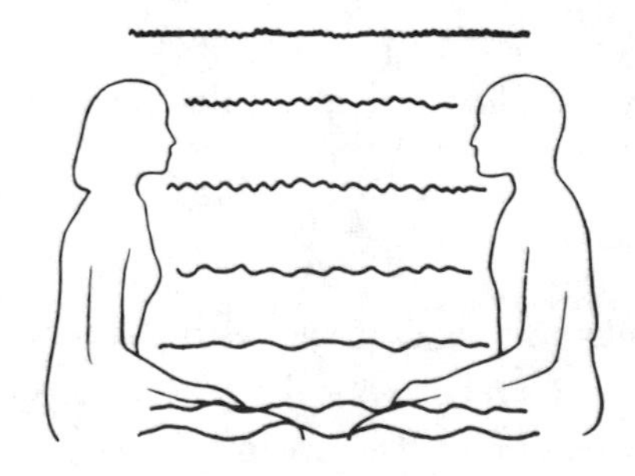

Connecting chakral energies

The Effects of Modern Society

Because of our highly technological society, we are all subject to intense, prolonged, and high vibrational fields which cannot help but affect the vibrations throughout our subtle body. This fact, in addition to the common use of mind-altering drugs and the easy availability of esoteric knowledge, means the ritualistic procedures that encouraged a gentle, gradual opening of our deep energy centers are being lost. The net result is that more people, either intentionally or unintentionally, are rapidly opening to their formative levels of body energy. This has disadvantages as well as advantages.

The main disadvantage is the increased potential for physical, mental, and spiritual discord. We are already seeing this, and groups such as the Spiritual Emergency Network[4] are being formed to disseminate information and provide professional guidance. More and more people are becoming aware, through personal experience and academic study, of the nature of these deep energetic shifts, and are learning to act as guides and teachers, providing support through difficult periods of transition. Because of the higher frequency vibrations of modern society, and our increasing distance from the natural rhythms of nature, I expect we will see kriya phenomena which will be of a different expression than have been experienced and reported in the past.

The advantage of the accelerated openings of these formative energies is new potential. If Gopi Krishna is correct in his belief that the kundalini process is a normal evolutionary force in humans, and if ascending the chakral ladder leads from competition to cooperation to wisdom, then the increasing exposure of people to these experiences may have a very positive effect. The inherent high vibrations of our society can give us more power to work with. As we learn to direct this in a healthy and creative way, we may ultimately discover that the cooperative merging of our high-tech society with ancient systems of knowledge is truly a catalyst for creating a better world.

4 Spiritual Emergency Network, California Institute of Transpersonal Psychology, 250 Oak Grove Avenue, Menlo Park, CA 94025 (415) 327-2776.

3
Foundations for The Energetic Bridge

The divorce between scientific facts and religious facts may not necessarily be eternal as it at first seems . . . the rigorously impersonal view of science might one day appear as having been a useful eccentricity rather than the definitely triumphant position which the sectarian scientist at present so confidently announces it to be.

– *William James*

Working with energy in a therapeutic context often seems "intangible" to the person accustomed to modern scientific methods. Like any phenomenon in modern physics, evidence for its existence is found only in its effects on phenomena in the environment around it; it cannot be "seen" in the ordinary sense. For example, although electricity cannot be seen with the naked eye, its presence becomes clear when it illuminates a light bulb or causes a motor to turn. We "experience" the presence of energy just as we experience other phenomena such as thoughts and feelings that also cannot be seen with the eyes or objectively measured.

When first learning to experience the movement, shape, and balance of energy as an entity that is distinct from the physical body, it is not unusual for people to doubt their own perceptions. Thoughts such as: "Am I really feeling this?" or "Is this really happening?" or "I must be imagining this," are not uncommon.

When first learning about working with energy it is helpful for the student to be in a supportive environment, with people who are as interested and sincere about learning as he or she is. Without the ability to communicate with other people who are going through similar experiences, one's own experiences will be harder to validate. If, for example, a student believes he or she has seen an auric field and is with people who have either never seen one or don't believe in the existence of auric fields, the student may discount his or her own experience, no matter how valid.

It is advantageous in learning about energy in the body to establish ground rules. A number of models, narratives of therapeutic experiences, definitions, principles, and guidelines are found in this chapter that will help the student of energy work do just that.

Much of the material found here was taken from the structural acupressure system known as "Zero Balancing." It should be understood that these exercises are not meant to stand alone, but are integral to a complete therapeutic system. They are taken out of the context of the Zero Balancing system only to provide people with examples of the ways we can experience energy.

Perceiving the Unseen

We have four natural gifts to perceive the unseen. These are *intuitive knowing, visionary seeing, prophetic foreseeing,* and *sensitive feeling.* Although we are all born with these abilities, only a few people learn skills for using them consciously and deliberately. With effort and training most people are capable of bringing one or more of these talents to the surface. Any one of them may be used to assess movement and energy within nature and within the human body, although each provides its user with somewhat different data about the nature of the energy. In this chapter, we will discuss material related to the natural gift of *sensitive feeling* and perceiving energy through our hands.

Energy Perception

Hands-Off Scanning:

Vibratory fields of the body extend beyond the physical boundaries. The distance and intensity vary according to the health and vitality of the person. If we bring a hand toward someone's body, we may sense warmth, vibration, density, or "cushioning" — a sense of an invisible buffer or field extending beyond their surface. Some people compare it to the experience of feeling the force fields of two magnets lined up against their opposite poles, though it is much softer and subtler in the body. This can occur at variable distances, usually from one to eight inches from the skin surface. At that level, if we then move the hand parallel to the body, we will feel fluctuations in the temperature and density of the cushion, or possibly tinglings in our palms.

When scanning keep the hand in motion. Energy fields are perceived as we move through their varying densities. It is important to move at the correct speed (perhaps six inches every several seconds) keeping the correct distance (one to eight inches, depending on where you feel the cushion), hold the hand relaxed, and keep the mind in a receptive mode.

A common exercise is to scan one's own body and then to scan another person and compare experiences. There are definite feelings and sensations involved from the point of view of the person doing the scanning and of the person being scanned.

Scanning is particularly useful in evaluating auric fields, chakras of the body, energy moving through meridian pathways, and the energy field just below the skin. In therapy, I often use scanning to balance these energy fields. In some therapeutic situations the hand moves in such a fashion as to encourage flow and balance; in other situations one or both hands may be held stationary over the patient, while the patient's energy orients around that area; and in other situations the hands may be positioned as two poles for the energy to bridge. Specific techniques vary according to therapeutic systems, the personal style of the therapist, and the energetic functions required.

Hands-On Palpation:

Energy fields permeate the physical body and we literally cannot touch a person without also encountering those fields. However, from the experiential viewpoint, we can touch the physical body without any *awareness* of being in contact with the energy itself. It is certainly common to be touched and yet have the feeling of being contacted only on the physical level. It is even possible to have an hour's massage and never be significantly contacted on the energetic level, where "essential touch" occurs.

Essential Touch

Essential touch is a basic concept. It means to be touched by or in touch with the *energy movement* of another person, animal, or object. It refers to the quality of the contact rather than to a method or technique. It is the experience of feeling "touched" in a significant way by another person, through a hug, a handshake, or through eye contact. May people describe it as an experience of feeling "connected" with another person in a way that transcends the physical contact itself.

The essential touch is a basic requirement in energy work. Most people agree that it is "much harder to describe than to do." It is a natural connection between people, and most people make such connections without being aware of them being special or "useful." A prime example of the essential touch occurs when a mother picks up a crying child and the child is quieted and comforted by the contact it experiences with the mother.

In the therapeutic situation, it is helpful to make this process conscious, to be aware of the experience of connecting and be able to have some choice about it. The paradox is that if we attempt to do this intellectually or from the position of the analytical mind, the connection tends to be blocked, that is, not to occur. The person who works with energy learns to make the use of essential touch "consciously instinctive"; it becomes the basic tool for accessing an energy field.

There are a number of sensations, mostly involving the feeling of movement or aliveness, which let us know we are engaging an energy field. We may perceive a fine vibration in the other person's body or in the aura, a feeling as if we were making contact with a low voltage current. This may be described as tingling, buzzing, a chill sensation, "goose bumps," as well as a subtle sensation that some people describe as "vibration." We may also perceive a grosser feeling of movement as though the person's body or our own were expanding or contracting, even though we see no physical change.

Think what it is like to stand or walk on a moving sidewalk of the sort found in airports. The sensation I have when I step onto the moving surface is akin to what I feel when I first encounter a person's energy. As I stand on the moving ramp, it is analogous to the feeling I have when I contact another person's energy movement from my own stillness. As I walk on the moving sidewalk, putting my body in motion, it is similar to the sensation I get when I relate to a person's energy body from my own movement or energy body.

Sometimes when we contact another person energetically, we have the feeling of "potential movement," that is, the presence of energy in a temporarily static state. If we lean against a tree with our physical body, our perspective is of something solid, immovable, and basically not "alive." But if we lean into a tree with our energy field as well, there is a feeling that the tree is alive, viable, and flexible. Even though we are physically unable to move the tree, we can almost feel it bend, responding to our lean.

A clinical example of this potential movement is in palpating a person's head. If we palpate on the physical level, it is like feeling a solid nonresponsive globe; if we palpate from an energetic perspective, the pliability is apparent. An affirmation of this is to feel a number of heads and experience that some are "softer" than others, and that on occasion one may actually feel "too hard."

Fulcrums: Creating Simple Bridges For Energy Assessment

> A "fulcrum" is a balance point: "A position, element, or agency through, around, or by means of which vital powers are exercised."
>
> — *American Heritage Dictionary*

The simplest fulcrum is created by the direct pressure of one or more fingers into the body to form a firm support, around which the body can orient. The fulcrum needs to be "deep" enough into the body so that the physical slack of the tissue is taken up; this is the point at which any further pressure meets with resistance in the tissue beneath your fingers. The basic principle is that we must "get in touch" with the person's energy body. This is done by taking up the slack from the physical body *so that any additional movement on our part will be translated directly into the person's experience.*

This principle could also be demonstrated by filling a balloon with water until it is ten or twelve inches in diameter. Rest it on a table and slip the fingers under it. Raise the fingers and be sensitive to the pressure at the fingertips. Note that in the first portion of the raise the slack of one's own tissue is absorbed as well as the slack of the balloon. Further pressure exerted will "connect" with the mass of water in the balloon. At that point the fingers will be acting as a fulcrum for the balloon. Once in touch with the balloon in this way the fulcrum can be held superficially or pressed deeper into the balloon by exerting more pressure with the fingers. At any fulcrum or balance point, one is in solid contact with the material, the mass orients around the finger, and any further pressure will affect the energy.

Fulcrums can be created in a number of ways. Besides the direct pressure with the fingers or hand, they can be developed through movements such as stretching, pressing, twisting, bending, or sliding.

A rubber band can illustrate stretching as a fulcrum. Pick up a rubber band and stretch it just far enough to take up the slack. Once this is done the rubber band has been "contacted," and any further movement will stretch the rubber itself.

In applying traction to a person's legs or neck, I often use what I call a "half-moon vector," which combines both lifting and pulling motions, which translates into a curved pull. All of these work on the same principle: once we have taken up the physical slack, we have established an interface, a fulcrum. Any additional movement on our part will be felt by the other person; any movement in the other person's body will be felt by us. We are in touch with his or her energy body.

Across this bridge we can then evaluate directly by feeling the movement present, the vibrations and currents, or by adding more movement, feeling how the body responds.

Fine Tuning of Fulcrums

While applying a fulcrum, I monitor myself by asking, "how is this feeling to the patient?" and, "how would this feel if this were being done to me?" Both of these lines of self-inquiry help to direct me to pull harder or softer, to twist more or less, and to establish the level of interaction and balance at which I can most fully connect with the person. Additionally, I may specifically ask the person how the force feels: would he or she like it altered to make it feel "better" or "more essential"? With a straight pressure-type fulcrum, an ideal working level is where the pressure "hurts good." This is what I call the "hedonic" level. It is fair to say that what feels good, right, or correct to the person will lead to a beneficial balance within the energy field.

Guidelines for Evaluation Through Touch

When we put our hands on another person and establish contact through essential touch, we have two physical bodies and two energy systems coming together. We need to distinguish between what we are perceiving of our own body and what we are perceiving of another person. Furthermore, we need to do this for both the physical body and the subtle body. The question to be asked at this point, is "What is mine and what is thine?"

Therapeutic Relationships

Four therapeutic physical-energetic relationships are possible. The therapist can evaluate the physical body (the particle, the stationary components) of the client or the energy body (the wave forms, the movement) from either his or her own physical body or his or her own energy body. Consider this analogy: as observers, we can stand looking at a stationary train, or stand still watching a moving train. We

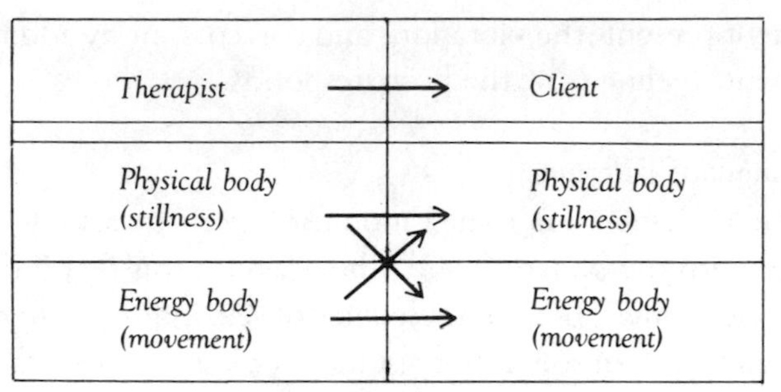

Four possible relationships of the therapist to the client

can be on a moving train watching the stationary countryside, or we can be on a moving train watching another moving train. A special situation exists in this last example when our train is moving in the same direction and at the same speed as the train we are watching. We have the illusion that we are stationary with the world around us in motion.

The least complicated relationship of therapist to a client is like the example of watching the train from a grounded vantage point. The viewer or examiner "remains stationary" and assesses either the static or the moving components of the other person.

The most complicated relationship between therapist and client is when the examiner attempts to evaluate the movement in the other person from his or her own moving base — like watching a passing train while standing inside another moving train. In that case, no one is grounded. If the therapist doesn't pay close attention, a lack of clarity and energetic confusion can result. If the energy systems of the client and therapist happen to come into phase or synch, the situation becomes even more confusing because — like the analogy of two trains going at the same speed — the illusion of stability will occur, when there is actually no stability at all.

The Perceiving Client

All the while the therapist is involved in his or her work, the client is perceiving the therapist, his or her adeptness, touch and interest. Whether the client does this consciously or unconsciously, information feeds into the client's personal data bank of experience and affects the degree of trust. This in turn directly affects the availability of the client's energy body to the therapist and the therapeutic process.

Energy "Disconnects"

Whether a therapist is simply doing energy exercises or actually engaging in energy assessment and balancing, there are important reasons to make periodic, frequent disconnects from the other person. If energy fields stay in contact too long, there is accommodation, and we lose the ability to either read or experience the difference between "them" and "us." A common example of the accommodation phenomenon is walking into a room where there is an odor. At first the odor may capture our attention, but after a short time has passed, we no longer smell it. As with smell, we accommodate quickly to energetic connections.

Another reason for frequent energetic disconnects is that with prolonged connections, one person may drain the energy from the other, much like when a battery is left connected to a light or other load.

Guidelines for Assessing Responses of The Energy Body

No two people are the same, and a number of responses are possible to an essential energetic connection.

Elongation

A frequent phenomenon is the feeling of elongation of the person's energy body. In Zero Balancing I often experience this when activating the central flow through the spine by means of applying leg traction. As I hold the traction constant, it may feel as though the person is elongating six, eight, ten inches, or more beyond their physical limit. This is most apparent when my eyes are closed. When viewed, the physical body reveals no change; *sensing* the energy body gives the impression that it is stretching into my hands. This *feeling* of extension may be accompanied by sensations of energy streaming into my hands. Once I am in touch with energy, I am in touch with the feeling of movement. As I maintain the traction, there usually comes a point where the elongation stops, and the limit of the energy body has been reached for the amount of traction exerted.

Extension

Having reached this limit, one of two possible phenomena will now occur. The first is that the client's body will seem to come to a rest at this extended position and remain quiet. If this happens, I gently diminish my traction on the energy body, then on the physical body, and place the legs back down on the table. Typically, the client will be extremely relaxed, usually in an altered state of consciousness. I give the person several moments to "come back" to normal consciousness, to savor the experience, and wait until he or she is fully "present" before moving on.

Contraction

The second response of the elongated energy body is to contract into itself and pull away from my hands. At this point I must decide whether to move with the rebound or to anchor it. Both of these responses will carry a person deeper into altered consciousness, more so with the anchoring than with the rebound.

Rebound

If I elect to go with the rebound, as the energy body retracts, I move with it, offering just enough resistance so that the retracting energy has something to pull against until it stops its flow. It is like letting a stretched rubber band slowly go back to its slack position, feeling the decreased stretch all the way until it is stable. Then I put the person's legs down.

Anchoring

If I choose to have the person explore the altered state of consciousness more deeply, I will anchor the rebounding energy body by holding the same amount of force on the legs. The sensation will be that the energy field is pulling away from me, and that the person is elongating in the opposite direction. It may seem as though the client extends several feet beyond the head end of the table. The process of anchoring requires a good deal of strength, for which I need to be prepared. Once this dynamic is set up, I wait until the other person's body comes back to the beginning point or "back into my hands," before I let the feet back down on the table.

Sometimes the energy body does not come back easily and stays in the elongated position; I can reverse this by adding a gentle stimulus: by squeezing my hands tighter, applying extra pull on the feet, or just quietly asking the person to return. When the energy field matches the physical body, I disconnect and allow the person to reorient.

Streaming

Occasionally, with traction on the lower extremities, the energy body will elongate and I will not feel it "stop" nor "rebound." Instead I will feel a continual "streaming" through my own body, and may experience my own shape change. In this situation, I have excessively grounded the person and have inadvertently entered into the person's energy experience, as the energy flows through me into the earth. We are both moving in the same direction (remember the train analogy), and there is no working interface. This can energetically deplete us. I ground my feet more fully, center my body, tighten my grip, and change the angle of the traction. This change of angle may be in any direction. If streaming continues, I make minute jerking motions, similar to setting the hook in a fish. Once the energy has been "seated," I establish an interface between the patient and myself, and continue to create my fulcrum.

Energetic Evaluation of the Subtle Body

The basic energy model presented in the first chapter consists of the conducted energy flows of the *vertical currents* of the Universal Life flow, uniting us to nature; the *internal energy flow* (deep, middle, and superficial) organizing us as individuals; and the *background field* permeating the whole being. These all blend as functions in the subtle body.

In the actual evaluation of these energy flows, however, the *tissues* through which they move are more relevant than the *function* of the flows. Therefore the discussion of the energetic assessment of our model will be based on the body tissue. Specifically, it will begin with energy currents in bone itself. The skeleton will then be considered in terms of the *freely movable joints* (the deep level of our internal energy system), and basic *foundation joints* (the vertical energy flows). Discussion of the soft tissue of the body (the middle and superficial layers of our internal flows) and the energy which exists freely in all body tissues (the background field) will follow. Finally, comments on assessing specific energy fields involving isolated joints will be included.

Assessment of the Bone

Reading energy currents and flows within the bone itself can most easily be demonstrated by evaluating the long bones of the body. There is a general axiom that no one is symmetrical. No two forearms will energetically feel the same. This can be easily demonstrated:

Take hold of a person's forearm above the wrist and below the elbow, and gently put a bending or "bow" movement into the arm.

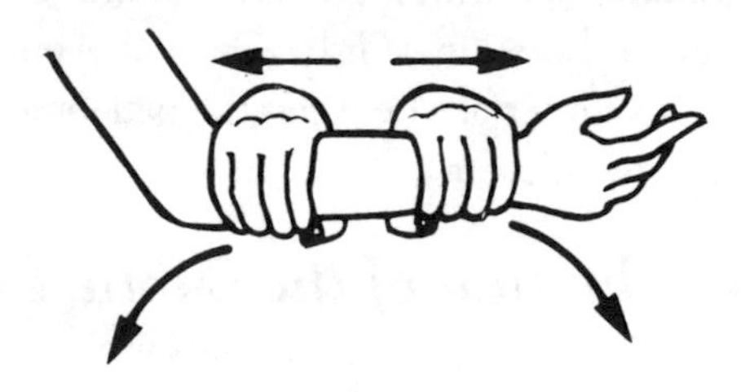

Energy currents in bone: take up slack and gently bow the forearm

After taking up the slack of the physical body and soft tissues, the resistance of the bone itself will be encountered. Make a bowing motion in one direction and then gently release this tension; then make a bowing motion in the opposite direction. Try this several times, once with the eyes open, and once with the eyes closed. Repeat the exercise on the person's other forearm and compare the findings.

In a "normal" uninjured extremity, the arm may bow more easily in one direction than the other; one bow may feel obstructed; or the bow may have the suggestion of a twisting motion. Similary, one forearm may feel like a steel bar while the other may feel like rubber.

In any assessment of the body there is great variation within the theoretical norm. We must each establish for ourselves a range of normalcy to determine what is an acceptable function or response. Broad guidelines can be taught, but each clinician must ultimately develop his or her own sense of the normal variations. Simple exercises, such as those with the forearm, help develop parameters.

A second exercise is to introduce a twisting motion in a long bone, as if gently wringing a sweater. This is most easily performed on the leg, as the natural rotational movement in the forearms confuses physical motion with the bone elasticity. Place one hand just above the ankle and the other hand below the knee. Take up slack in the soft tissue and gently twist in one direction, feeling the bony resistance. Repeat in the opposite direction.

Because the bones are denser in the leg than in the forearm, and because the muscles are heavier, it takes a moment longer to perceive the energy currents interacting with the twisting motion. It is an exaggeration to say that energy on this level moves with the speed of molasses, but the principle is true.

Do this exercise with several people. Experience three or four variations in a short time, and then compare experiences with each other. Sharing experiences validates perceptions and gives them authenticity, plus allowing exposure to other possibilities.

In early energy training, the issue is not to judge something as good or bad, normal or abnormal, but rather to describe the experience to oneself so that one can become sensitive to what one is feeling under one's hands. This is enhanced by being "worked on" by other people, experiencing one's own body, and perceiving the varieties of touch. To never receive body therapy or massage is to miss one of the most profound lessons in body energy.

Healed Fractures

The evaluation of energy movement through healed fractures of the long bones of the body gives further insight into energy currents. The energy field across fractures may feel heavy and dense, have low vitality, or be disorganized and chaotic. These qualities are related to the process of reconnecting or bridging the energy fields across the damaged bone. Of course, the more severe the initial injury, the greater possibility there will be of having distorted energy fields. Yet some people with severe fractures end up with an energetically harmonic bone.

Invariably, when I bring up this subject at seminars, people ask if chaotic or low-vitality energy fields around previously broken bones can be improved. The answer is that usually they can. Improvement is affected by introducing force fields stronger than the fields in the existing bone, and holding them for a moment.

For instance, with a healed forearm fracture, I would first evaulate the currents, as in the bowing exercises. If indicated, I would balance the fields by grasping the arm above the wrist and below the elbow, and take up the slack by stretching apart my hands. Holding this, I might add a further stretching force, and then, in addition, a bowing and/or a twisting force. I hold this configuration, being sensitive to the resilience of the bone, for a brief period of time, possibly fifteen to twenty seconds, and then gently release.

On reevaluation I should notice a lessening of the asymmetry of the original force fields, and a greater freedom of energetic movement through the long bone. I allow myself three maneuvers for change to occur or to create the maximum shift in any one session.

Assessment of Skeletal Energy: Vertical Flow

The Universal Life flow of energy enters the skeleton through the head, flows downward through the cranial bones, the intervertebral and costovertebral joints, down the spine to the sacroiliac, through the legs to the metatarsals, and out the feet into the earth. The parallel flows enter the top of the shoulder girdle, flow along the edges of the transverse processes, and join the Universal Life flow in the pelvis. The flows also move through the shoulder girdle and out to the hands. These vertical flows are evaluated through two special groups of joints: the foundation and semi-foundation joints.

Foundation Joints

This group of joints includes the cranial bones of the skull, the sacroiliac articulation, the intratarsal articulations of the foot, the intracarpal articulations of the hand, and the pubic symphysis. The foundation joints deal with the transmission and balance of mechanical and energetic forces in the body rather than with the movement and locomotive components of the musculo-skeletal system. They are directly involved with the lightning rod currents conducted through the spine.

All the foundation joints have a *small range of motion*. It is so small in some cases that there is argument that it exists at all. The mainstream teaching in Western science is that there is no movement of the bones in the adult's skull. However, a growing minority of physicians, led by the cranial osteopaths, believe that the cranial bones not only move, but that balanced movement is critical for optimal body function.

There is also disagreement regarding movement in the sacroiliac joint. Some medical books say there is no movement; some say that there is movement, but the movement has no significance; some say that the sacroiliac joint moves only during childbirth; still others say this is the most significant joint in the pelvic mechanism. Interestingly, most anatomy texts indicate the sacroiliac joints have characteristics of a *freely movable joint*.

The More Important Foundation Joints

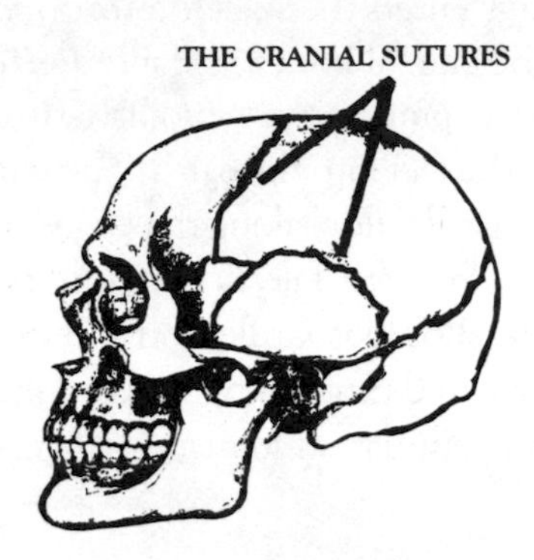

CRANIAL JOINTS OF THE SKULL

SACROILIAC JOINTS AND THE PUBIC SYMPHASIS OF THE PELVIS

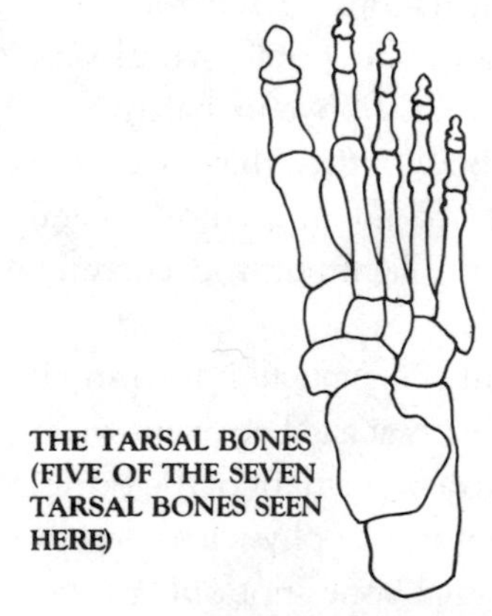

THE INTERTARSAL JOINTS OF THE FOOT

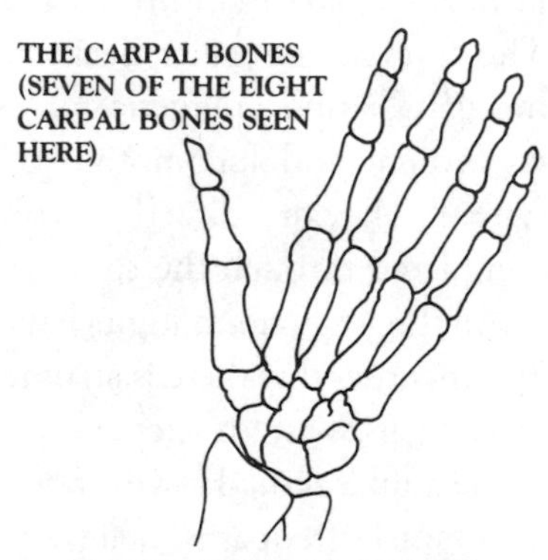

THE INTERCARPAL JOINTS OF THE HAND

An important characteristic of these joints is that there is *no voluntary motion*. Voluntary motion in a joint is made possible by muscles whose tendons span a joint. The foundation joints have ligaments and /or fascial tissue spanning the joint surfaces but no muscle structure. The movement which does occur is as a response to forces *acting upon* the area rather than being initiated by the part itself; the movement is outside or beyond our conscious control.

Because of the lack of voluntary motion, when there is an imbalance or altered function of these joints, the body tends to *compensate for the problem,* rather than resolving it. The compensatory process is widespread, and involves other structures associated with the joint involved. These patterns of compensation tend to become locked into the body, limiting other functions and potentials.

Because of the ligament /fascial anatomy of the foundation joints, the motion which does occur is fully within the end point of motion range. The ligaments are under constant tension and any limitation of motion is a direct read-out of the energetic component of the joint. Of all joints in the body, these have the closest relationship to the subtle body.

Semi-Foundation Joints

The semi-foundation joints are a subcategory of the foundation joints. The more important of these are the intervertebral articulations, and the joints of the ribs (costovertebral, costotransversus, and costosternoid). The less (energetically) important are the articulations of the clavical with the sternum and with the first rib.

These joints have many of the same characteristics as the foundation joints. They still have a small range of motion, although significantly larger than the foundation joints. They are beyond our level of voluntary control, even though there may be direct muscle connections. For instance, muscles do bridge from one vertebra to its neighbor, and these muscles are activated when we move the spinal column as a whole. However, to specifically contract the muscle group between any two vertebrae, say lumbar three and four, as an isolated motion, is almost impossible. Even to locate in the mind the junction between lumbar three and lumbar four is a major achievement in physical awareness!

The remaining characteristics of this group are similar to those of foundation joints. They also serve as a bridge between the physical and subtle anatomy, and the evaluation of their end points of motion give us direct information about the deeper mechanisms of the individual.

The More Important Semi-foundation Joints

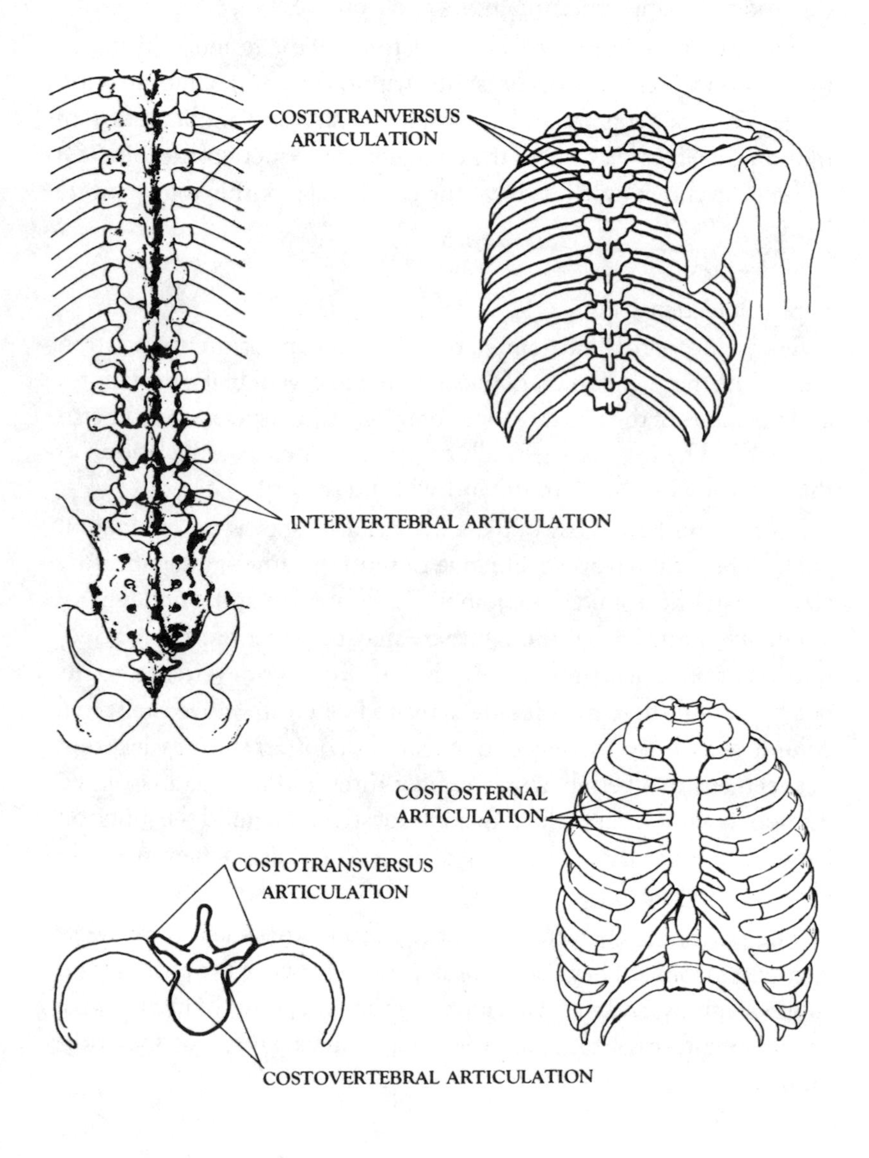

Assessment of Skeletal Energy: Deep Level of the Internal Flow

The skeleton incorporates all the joints in the body as a single, integrated unit. It is through the joints rather than the isolated bones, that we derive information about the deep level flow of the internal energy system. In the course of walking and moving, the generated force fields move through the joints in the skeleton in two major ways: a portion arcs directly across the joint space between the bone ends, and a portion is conducted through the supporting ligaments. To understand the implications of these flows it is necessary to review joint physiology and, in particular, joint play, the range of motion, and the end point of motion for joints.

Joint Play

There is a subtle aspect of joint movement, called "joint play" which is outside the range of voluntary control and can be evaluated only through passive motion. Joint play is a certain looseness in the joint that is vital: without it we would have a frozen, immovable structure; with too much looseness, we would have an unstable mechanism.

The concept of joint play is discussed in the books of John Mennell, M.D. (see bibliography). To demonstrate joint play, stretch any finger from the knuckle and feel the looseness. Then passively move the finger in any direction and notice that there is looseness in all planes.

Muscles cannot contract fully unless there is a slight give in the joint beyond the full muscle contraction. With impairment of joint play, not only is the joint itself jeopardized, the muscles cannot function normally. These secondary effects on the muscles activating the joint ultimately can lead to problems within the muscle tissue itself.

From the energetic viewpoint, the space of the joint play adds to the resilience of the joint and acts as a cushion and shock absorber between the bony or cartalaginous surfaces. Gently separating and compressing the bone ends of a joint will reveal this cushion and give information to the interface of physical structure and the energy flow across the bone ends. If the gap is too thin, energy arcs the space too easily; if it is too full, the energy flow is inhibited.

Range of Motion

Every freely movable joint of the body has a normal "range of motion" (ROM) which is under voluntary control. In a typical Western medical examination, we evaluate these motions in both an active and passive manner. To wit: we ask the patient to bend, straighten, or rotate a joint, and note whether or not it has a normal range of motion. We may then have the patient relax while me move the joint passively through its range to again gain insight into any limitations of joint function.

If there is a limitation of the range of motion, one of the skills of the Western medical practitioner is to evaluate the cause of the limitation, be it a local problem within the joint and its supportive soft tissues, a problem with the neuromuscular bundles activating the joint, a problem of the supply systems (blood, nerves, lymph) to the joint, a problem in the central nervous system of the body, or in the blood chemistries. The differential diagnosis of restrictions of ROM is broad.

End Point of Motion of the Joints

Beyond the voluntary range of joint motion is the "end point of motion" (EPM). The end point of motion is a function of the ligaments of the joint and is a reflection of the energy contained in and passing through the ligaments. The EPM constitutes that portion of the motion from where we first begin to feel resistance, as the soft tissues limit the movement, to where we reach the limit of motion. The term "end point of motion" does not mean the final billionth of an inch, at which point the joint can no longer move; it refers to that portion of the motion from where the tissues first engage in stopping the motion. In physiotherapy, the end point of motion is known as the *end feel* of joint junction.

End point of motion of a joint is evaluated through *passive motion*, and is a readout of the ligaments. They, not the muscles, limit joint movement and there is a characteristic feeling as the ligaments begin to engage: gradual, smoothly increasing resistance with a firm but yielding quality is felt in a healthy ligament until no further passive motion is possible. With less well-functioning ligaments there may be an abrupt, sudden stop within the end point of motion. Or, if the joint is too loose, there may be little feeling of tissue resistance. No two joints are ever the same, even within the same person.

Flexing the wrist forward and then gently pressing down on the knuckles with the opposite hand gives a feeling of that softness and pliability typical of an end point of motion. A different end point feel is expressed by fully extending the elbow, where in full extension one bone seems to lock into another, and we have an abrupt bone-to-bone feeling as the joint reaches its limits. Yet even within that abrupt end point, on a subtle level one can still feel the yielding quality in the ligaments.

In reading a joint's end point of motion, it is unnecessary and undesirable to take the joint to its farthest extreme stopping position. Whenever we take a person beyond his or her usual frame of reality, whether this is on the level of the joint function or on the emotional, psychological, or spiritual level, it is easy to imprint negatively as well as to stimulate creatively. Imprints which occur in extreme positions are difficult to remove, because they are beyond the level of normal, everyday consciousness. Therapy is often needed to resolve imbalances which extend to the end points because the problem lies beyond the person's own ability to reach it.

ROM/EPM Compared

It is very important to make a clear distinction between the range of motion and the end point of motion of a joint. The ROM is that movement which we can voluntarily initiate in any joint, and which towards its extreme begins to engage the ligaments. It can be measured through active or passive motion. The EPM is a function of the ligament and is the joint motion beyond which the ligaments begin to limit or stop the range of movement; it can only be evaluated through

Joint Motion

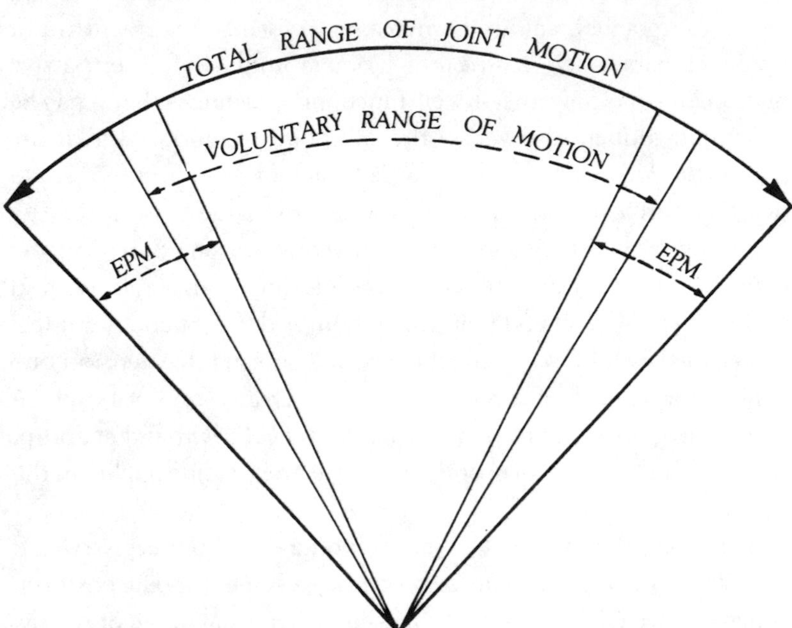

The voluntary range of motion and the end point of motion (EPM) in relation to the total range of joint motion

passive movement. That portion of the EPM which is beyond the ROM can be considered beneath our level of consciousness; it is primarily the energy contained in and channeled by the ligaments.

Disturbance of the EPM is often asymptomatic, but is an early sign of future degenerative changes. And this type of limitation does not show itself through voluntary range of motion, or X-ray examination. It is a determination made by the passive examination of the joint motion. The EPM can often be improved by manually introducing a stronger force field through the joint, using the method previously described for improving the energy flow in a healed fracture. Any improvement which is made in the involuntary portion of joint motion will help reduce pain, if present, and lessen the tendency toward future degenerative changes.

Assessment of Soft Tissue Energy: Middle Level of Internal Flow

This component of the subtle body is "where we live." It has the closest connection to our personal needs and to our emotional/mental responses to the world. Almost every type of therapy affects this level.

Evaluating energy movement through the soft tissues of the physical body is quite different than evaluating the movement of energy through the bone. It is difficult to take up enough slack from the soft tissue itself to allow us to directly read the energy currents. The most common way of evaluation is to feel the resistance (or lack of resistance) to movement as one passes the fingers or hands through the soft tissue. The muscle tension one feels during massage, or the fascial tension during Rolfing, are common examples.

Soft tissue currents themselves are easier to read by making two energetic contacts with our fingers and reading the current as it flows from one point to the other. For example: with the finger of one hand, press into the tissue below the elbow and make an essential connection. With the other hand, make a similar soft tissue connection above the wrist. Hold these two points and wait until the sense of connection is felt between the two fingers. This feeling of contact may be manifest as pulsation, movement, buzzing, or a sense that the fingers are directly connected through the other person's body.

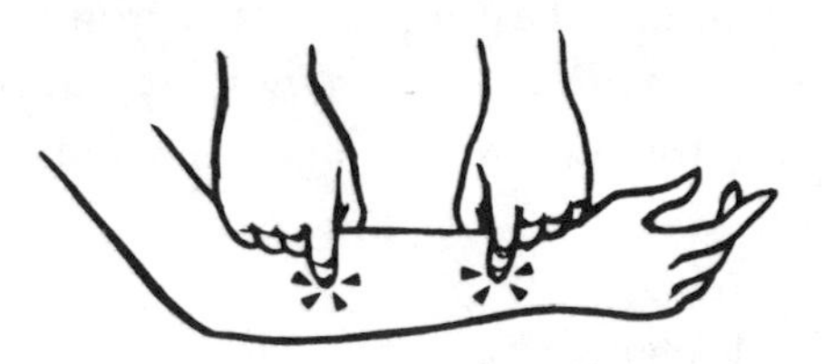

Soft tissue currents: hold two points of contact

Evaluate the time it takes for the circuit to complete as well as the strength and quality of the current itself.

There is disagreement among energy workers as to whether the right hand always sends energy and the left hand always receives, and whether it is important to use the right or left hand in a particular sequence. My personal experience is that energy follows thought and that either hand can be used to send or receive; the energy will follow whichever thought pattern one establishes, left to right or right to left. In the type of soft tissue evaluation which we are now considering, my personal preference is to let both hands be "neutral" and to allow the person's body to organize itself around my two poles, following the principle of the fulcrum.

Traditional Chinese Medicine Assessment

There are a number of other ways to access, evaluate, and balance the middle energy layer. One of the most detailed and sophisticated is the system of acupuncture and Traditional Chinese Medicine (TCM), a portion of which involves the sense of touch.

The core of diagnosis in Traditional Chinese Medicine is based on four areas of interrogation and examination: asking, seeing, listening, and feeling. The evaluator inquires into the nature of a person's complaint, clinical history, and family history, much as we do in taking a medical history in Western medicine. On less apparent levels the evaluator looks for the color the patient manifests, "listens" to the quality of vibration in the voice, "smells" the odors of the body, all of which provide insights into that state of the body's energy balance. In terms of feeling, or touch, the evaluator goes beyond palpation of the body as we know it; he or she feels for energy related to acupuncture points and meridian pathways, to skin and tissue, and to the traditional Chinese pulses.

The Pulses of Traditional Chinese Medicine

One of the many differences between TCM and Western medicine is the concept of pulses. TCM teaches there is a specific pulse for each of the twelve major, paired energy pathways and their associated organs or functions. These twelve pulses are most frequently measured on the radial artery, six on the right wrist and six on the left. They may also be felt over the carotid artery in the neck and the artery in the ankle.

In my personal study of TCM, these twelve "Chinese pulses" initially were a dilemma for me, as the concept was so foreign to my medical training. After I learned to *feel* and use them, though, they became further evidence to me that the energy network of acupuncture truly exists. Clinically the pulses are reliable when evaluating a problem, selecting a treatment, and determining whether the treatment selected was adequate and successful.

Information gained through the TCM diagnosis is interpreted by means of various grids. These include the five elements (metal, water, wood, fire, and earth), the twelve organs and functions (lungs, colon, kidneys, bladder, liver, gall bladder, heart, small intestines, pericardium, triple warmer, spleen, and stomach) and the eight conditions (yang/yin, exterior/interior, hot/cold, excessive/deficient).

Treatment in TCM may involve acupuncture (needles and moxibustion), herbs, massage, breathing practices, and physical exercises (often related to martial arts). With the exception of herbs, establishing an energetic connection with the patient or with oneself is a basic requirement for these therapies.

Assessment of Soft Tissue: Superficial Level of Interal Flow

The superficial layer of energy is called "wei chi," or the "protective chi," in traditional Chinese medicine. It is described as a coarse, diffuse energy beneath the skin that acts as a buffer or insulator.

This energy can be most directly assessed by scanning the energy fields with the hands, just off the surface of the body, and by palpating the texture and temperature of the skin. One can stimulate the wei chi through activities such as cold showers, use of a loofa (a large, abrasive, organic sponge), or with a body brush. I have seen people who were excessively vulnerable or sensitive to their external environment greatly benefit through daily stimulation of the wei chi in these ways.

Assessment of the Background Field of Energy

Underlying the organized energy fields through the bone, in the soft tissue, and beneath the skin is the background energy field of the body. This field permeates the body at all levels and extends beyond the physical limits into the surrounding space. Vibrations in this field represent part of the "background music" of an individual.

The vibration and movement within this "media" resonate with our internal and external environments, to our emotions, thoughts, and moods. It is sensitive to the needs, actions, and stance of our body/mind/spirit. All of these influences are the normal, everyday changes, and in the well-functioning system, the background energy fields move *with* this fluctuation, absorbing and releasing the vibrations and movements with equal ease. These events are not imprinted on the field beyond the moment of the influence.

Imprinting

However, it is possible to imprint more deeply on the field and thus leave a vibration or movement, with a resultant imbalance. These imbalances are reflected as freestanding energy wave forms, abnormal currents, vortices, or an excess or deficiency of energy within the field. They have nothing to do with the here-and-now or the needs of the body, but instead are reflections of past or perceived future events (fear or tension about an anticipated ordeal). These imbalances are generally the result of very forceful, often sudden, trauma or stimulus to the person, be it physical, chemical, emotional, or psychic, which is not absorbed by some other specific tissue or energy system.

Imprinting on the energy fields is more likely when the trauma is associated with heightened energy at the time of the impact. Specifically, the chances of imprinting are greater when the physical trauma occurs along with an emotional trauma, or when a person is in a highly excited, emotional state such as fear or anger or when the energy fields are depleted and lack resilience, as in times of depression, poor nutrition, or excessive fatigue. The combination of different simultaneous stresses increases the disruption of the subtle body. A significant trauma during this time of heightened or altered vibration may remain while the body calms back to normal. This is analogous to clothes in a dryer which are left to cool in a wrinkled position. The wrinkle may stay in the fabric. Sometimes that wrinkle will disappear when the garment is worn, and at other times the material must be reheated and then ironed out. In our bodies, some of the imprinting resolves itself just by the movements in our body during the normal course of a day. But at other times the body needs to have the level of the vibration raised to "iron out" the energetic wrinkles. One way to increase the energy vibration is to induce a stronger energy field by means of properly applied traction or compression.

Assessment

We have two tasks when assessing the energy configurations within the background field. The first is to quiet the physical body so that we can feel the deeper energy patterns. The second task is to "take up the slack" in the energy field itself, so that we can perceive any predominant wave form. We can do this by means of a traction fulcrum through the legs or by using a compression fulcrum through the shoulders.

To reach the background fields through the shoulders, I sit at the head of the table, rest my hands firmly and comfortably over the person's shoulders, and gently press down toward the feet, compressing the body to the point of energetic contact.

As I gently push down on the shoulders toward the feet, the body will move beneath my hands until it reaches its compression limit for the amount of pressure I am applying. In doing this I have taken up the slack. Having engaged the physical body fully, I add slight pressure, which establishes my connection with the energy fields. When I have made good contact with the energy field, I just hold the pressure. If there are abnormal waves in that area, I am able to feel the sensations from the person's body in my hands.

Balancing the Background Energy Field

There are various ways of reducing or removing aberrant vibratory patterns from the general energy field of the body. One is to override them with a stronger, clearer energy field. Another is to introduce a force field which matches the aberrant pattern and hold it. If it is a close match, the abnormal pattern will diminish and resolve. The third method is to make an essential connection with the aberrant pattern itself, and anchor it as the energy body tries to pull away. It is not unusual to find immediately after applying these energy balancing techniques that the problem is still evident. When we reevaluate several weeks later, however, we may find the original patterns either gone or greatly reduced, and the client may state he or she feels much better. For long-standing patterns, a number of sessions may be required to relieve the problem.

A Clinical Example

I had the opportunity to examine a gentleman who, thirteen months before, had sustained injury in an auto accident in which his car rolled over an embankment. He had been under medical care, was found to be free of any significant bodily injury other than bruising, and yet had been in daily pain since the accident. Examining him, I did not find any cause for his pain within the physical body, or in the end points of joint motion. Nor did I find significant problems through a Traditional Chinese medical diagnosis to account for his pain. When I examined the background energy field, however, I found a strong twisting current extending from the right side of his chest to the left side of his abdomen. This flow through the trunk represented the imprinting from the twisting force to which the body was subjected as the car rolled down the embankment.

Once I felt the torquing energy currents, I remained in touch with that field and exerted a slightly stronger force field through his body by increasing my traction on his legs. Holding this stronger field, I had the sensation of a rebounding effect along the energy imprint itself. By anchoring the new field, I let the rebounding subside. When it was complete, I gradually released my hold in the energy body, then the physical body, and then rested his legs on the table. Immediately after this Zero Balancing, the man felt a great sense of grounding and quietness. When I examined him again two days later, he reported he had been free of pain since the treatment and felt internal calm and well being. Checking the energy field, I found that the twisting currents were gone. I know from experience that stronger patterns are imprinted in different degrees of indelibility, and that a number of balancing sessions are often required for their improvement.

As imprints are removed from the energy body, recollection of past events associated with the original injury often take place. Imprinting of vibration in the body is one basis for the phenomena of muscle memory. Where these vibrations are released from entrapment, recollection indicates successful treatment.

Once, while examining and treating a patient, I came across an indentation in the energy body at waist level. It was the type of asymmetry that might have been caused by a side blow. I asked him if he had ever received a blow in this area, and he said no. The next day he reported that later in the evening he had remembered a specific event. While playing high school football, he had jumped to receive a pass and while in midair was struck by an opponent's shoulder just above the waist, where I had detected the indentation. He made the observation that once one has left the ground to receive a pass one is totally committed, which he was when he received the trauma. He clearly recalled that as he was hit, he said to himself, "I will never allow myself to be vulnerable again." He had forgotten this entire experience until the night after the treatment.

Further discussion brought additional relevant information to light. In the past twenty years (he was forty-two years old), he had had difficulty in his personal relationships and particularly in developing emotional closeness and deep intimacy with his partner. This inability had led to the dissolution of a number of relationships. I saw this man six months later and he said that since the treatment he had found himself to be more "vulnerable" and his current relationship had improved markedly. He was more open to his partner and closer than ever before. It was as if the injunction he had given himself at the time of the football injury "never to be vulnerable again" had spilled over into his entire emotional life. Since the energetic imprinting had been released, the injunction seemed deactivated and his daily emotional life had made a quantum shift toward improvement.

Review of Principles

Several principles are illustrated by this case. The first is that if a person receives a trauma when he or she is already in a state of physical motion, it tends to imprint more than if the trauma is received when the recipient is stationary. During the motion, the energy body is stretched, and if it is hit in this configuration, the vibration may be locked in as the energy body retracts.

Any time we are subjected to trauma, when our general energy field is in a state of turmoil because of other stresses such as divorce, death in the family, or recovery from serious illness, the imprinting imposed leaves a more complicated pattern to resolve.

Another principle is that the effect of any blow depends on the area of the body which is hit. If the blow results in a general contusion in a nonspecific area, the imprinting will be in the general energy field. If the impact were directly over a meridian, the injury could go deeper into the system. If a person were hit over a solid organ such as the spleen, it could rupture. If the blow lands on a joint or long bone, a fracture or bony injury may occur. Of course, more than one or two levels of injury can occur at the same time.

In ancient China, a distinction was made between a "horse kick injury" and a "camel kick injury." A horse kick injury typically resulted in an area of acute trauma, severe at the onset, with healing following over a period of days or weeks. A similar impact from a camel kick often seemed mild at first, but gradually moved deeper, resulting in increasing symptoms over the coming weeks and months, involving the body both somatically and psychosomatically.

The energy from the hard horse hoof is absorbed directly into the physical body, stays local, and evokes immediate physical response. The energy from the softer camel hoof melds more into the recipient's body, smolders without stimulating the body's defense mechanism, and disperses through the energy systems to the viscera and psyche.

Assessment of Specific Energy Fields

We can assess specific areas or energy fields as well as general ones. Frequently in knee injuries of the type in which there is a side blow or "bumper" injury, it often seems as if the energy body has been "knocked off the track" of the physical body. Assume that a person has experienced a significant impact to the outside of the knee, not strong enough to cause damage that would show up in a medical diagnosis. The time of the injury may have been months or years prior to the examination. In these cases, the gross physical examination and X-rays are usually normal, though the person may have feelings of discomfort, aching, and instability of the knee.

Beyond the typical medical examination, I evaluate the energy of the knee by placing my hands on either side of the joint and pay attention to the feelings under each hand. If there has been a blow to the outside of the knee, the feeling beneath the outside hand will often give the sensation of an indentation, emptiness, lack of vitality, and perhaps coolness. The feeling under the inside hand is one of fullness, perhaps protrusion, and possibly slight warmth.

"Sometimes it seems as if the energy body has been 'knocked off the track' of the physical body."

I place my hands on the inside and outside of the thigh, and with firm contact, slide the hands down the thigh across the inner and outer surface of the knee onto the lower leg. Often, the feeling is that both sides of the thigh are the same — symmetrical, pleasantly warm, and full. As the hands move down, the outside hand will feel a gradual emptiness occurring as it approaches the knee, then fullness returning as it continues down the leg. The reverse will be true for the inside hand. It is as if the currents of energy flowing down the thigh have been "pushed off course" at the inside of the knee and then come back on course above and below it.

An additional way I can evaluate such an injury is to hold both hands approximately three-quarters of an inch off the physical body at mid-thigh, and then move them slowly down, scanning the fields. Again, sensations of emptiness and coldness on the outside hand and fullness and warmth on the inside are common.

The principle of treatment for this distorted energy field is similar to those presented earlier. I introduce a stronger energy field through the knee by applying gentle traction to the slightly flexed knee, establishing an essential touch with the energy field, and by holding the fulcrum for fifteen to twenty seconds. I can also press my hands on either side of the knee and, working directly with the energy of the knee, allow the field to stabilize between my hands, and then guide it back to the correct pattern.

Conclusion

There are many ways to detect and work with the energy fields within the body. One inherent advantage of using our hands in energy work is that the sense of touch, for most people, has a confirming quality. We trust what we can feel, and this adds an element of tangibility to the experience.

It takes practice to develop a sense of touch for making contact with the energy body, and for many people this is not fully confirmed until they can get feedback from others. It is possible, however, to get direct feedback of energy movement by watching the response of the client. In the next chapter we will explore some of these objective signs and describe what they indicate in terms of the energy body.

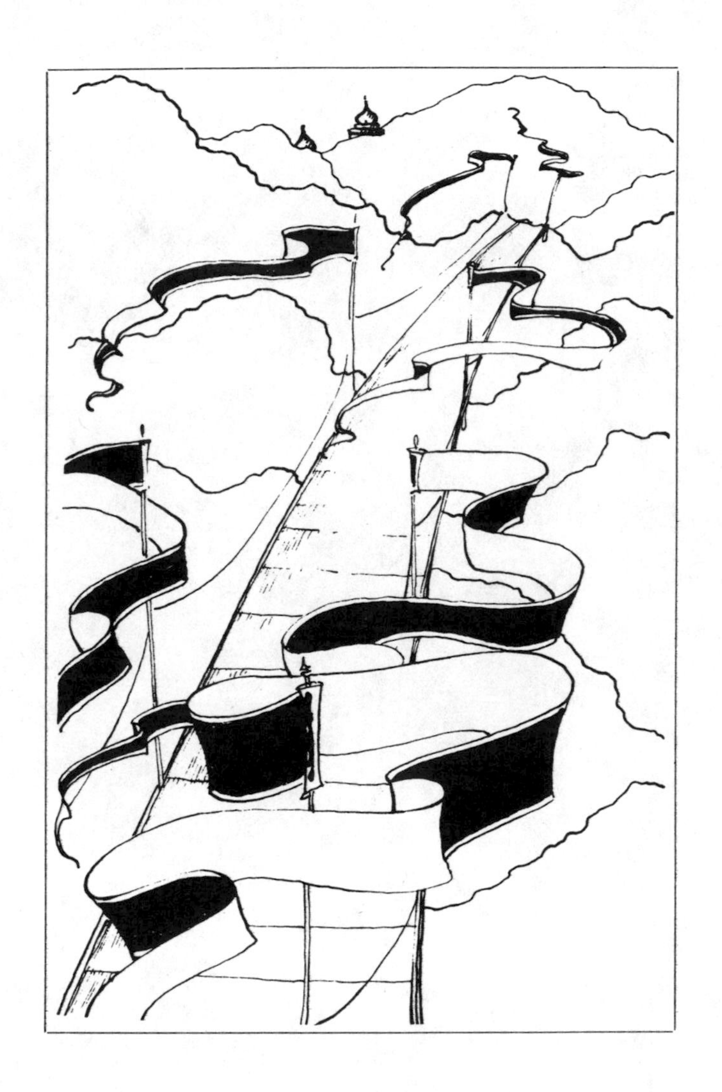

3

Bridges of Response

A person cannot not react.

After observing many energy balancing and body handling treatments, including acupuncture, Zero Balancing, acupressure, Feldenkrais, massage, and meditation, I realized that there were specific responses, as part of the experience, that appeared to be common to all these systems. It became clear that these responses resulted from the actual internal process of the recipient and that by understanding them one could monitor their actual process.

My interest in these responses and their implications began long before I was aware of the world of energy and vibration. It was only after I began to integrate the teachings of the East with the West that I understood that these responses occurred only when the energy body was specifically contacted. They were part of a general response to the essential touch.

Definitions of Criteria and Principles

Before outlining these observations it is important to define special criteria and principles I use in working with the subtle body.

Split Level of Awareness

I split my awareness when doing energy work. This is a familiar state of mind in everyday life: it occurs whenever we are involved in two or more activities at the same time. For example, while driving a car, part of our awareness is on operating the car, while another part of our consciousness may be looking at the scenery, thinking about work or home, or listening to the radio. We would have trouble if we tried to do all these things simultaneously through a single level of awareness. By allowing our awareness to fragment, we are able to handle different banks of data simultaneously.

When working with the subtle body, our main attention, our energy, is focused on our essential touch, and secondarily, on observing and sensing any reaction of the client.

Energetic connections can be lost if our thoughts drift or are focused elsewhere. Energy follows thought. If we focus on observing the client, we tend to lose the energetic bridge established through our hands. If, on the other hand, we learn to "split" our level of awareness, we can handle a dual input of information and still maintain our essential connection.

Witness State of Observation

In split-level awareness if one portion of the mind is used as an objective observer, it is called the "witness." The witness state implies that the observer is in a state of total objectivity while viewing the events. The witness is uncritical, nonjudgmental, expectation-free, and uninvolved with an active thought process. The witness does not affect the process or interact with the environment. There is no energetic connection.

When using this witness viewpoint, we actually pick up more information from the client than if we were to focus our attention and wait for some specific event to occur. There are many possible responses in any situation, and if we look too closely for one we may miss another. The energetic response can be visual, olfactory, auditory, vibrational, and so on. In the witness state, we can monitor a number of reactions simultaneously without significantly altering the course of events. We don't know ahead of time how an individual will respond to the movement of ch'i, but if we know the map of the territory, whatever the response, we will already know its significance and can use it to guide our interaction. Our witness does not need to "figure out" any meanings in the moment and run the risk of losing the energetic connection.

The witness state implies the use of "soft eyes." The principle of soft eyes is to let the information *come* to us rather than *reaching out* to it or staring ("hard eyes"). We all know the feeling of being "stared at." There is an energy field which develops as we project sight in this way that affects the recipient and influences the event. Using soft eyes allows us to gain information without being obtrusive or offsetting the outcome.

The Working State

We assume the normally resting body is in a state of relative equilibrium or homeostasis. Of course, our bodies are continually in a state of change and movement, but we are rarely aware of the thousands of small subliminal alterations that are regularly occurring. When the physical body and the energy body are in harmony, there is an experience of "balance." When we stimulate an energy flow and change its movement within the body, there will be internal shifts as the person adjusts to those changes and establishes new equilibrium. This period of internal rearrangement to an energetic shift is what I call the "working state," and means that the body/mind/spirit is responding, reorganizing, and reintegrating during or following a shift of balance or vibration.

Altered States of Consciousness

A person in the working state often has an altered state of perception. There may be feelings of deep serenity and calmness. The person may experience changes in body shape, feelings of floating or being outside of the body, or even feel as if he or she is disappearing. Time / space is often distorted; a fifteen minute experience may seem to have taken two or three hours or one to two minutes.

These altered perspectives and the distortion of time / space are not disturbing because they are actually cut from the same cloth as our daily life experience. The distortion of time and space is common to all of us: how quickly a good movie passes, how slowly a dull lecture. The same time / space distortion occurs when we drive a familiar distance; suddenly, we arrive in the driveway and cannot recall the trip home.

The working state has a special significance in energy balancing therapies. This is one of the times that healing tends to occur. When a person is in an altered state of awareness, he or she is removed from the ordinary mind set, which, among other things, contains a conceptualization of the imbalance. Any conception, vision, or neurological imprint of an imbalance tends to solidify the problem and give it form. If the mind set is altered *at the same time* we are providing the body / mind / spirit with the experience of being in a better state of balance (i.e., the fulcrum), there is an energetic and experiential reprogramming of the imbalance or illness. A degree of healing has occurred.

Our witness may observe that a client is in the working state, even though afterward the client may not recall a specific feeling or experience. It is very common for these shifts of the body / mind / spirit to take place subliminally, and to be detectable by the outsider but not recalled by the individual. If we have observed the signs of an energetic shift (the working state), we know there has been an effect regardless of the client's conscious experience or recall.

Principles of Change and Inertia

There are two paradoxical laws of nature. One law states: "Everything is in a state of change." The other, the law of inertia, states that it is inherent in things not to change, that is, "something will continue to move in the same direction until acted upon by an outside force."

Early in my training of manipulative therapy I was taught to "change an articulation." If a person was in trouble with a joint problem for which manipulation was indicated, the principle involved was to add a force to the joint which would directly alter the relationships of the involved structure. Even though manipulations are very effective, as I began to understand the principles of movement from the energetic viewpoint, other options to the manipulative approach became apparent.

Assume an imbalance within a joint. When I place a fulcrum into the joint, establish an essential connection, and hold it stationary in that balance, I am creating a situation of *no change* on both the physical and energetic level. As I maintain the state of balance and prohibit change, I challenge the body with the principle of "things always change." Something will begin to shift in relation to the fulcrum. I am forcing movement and an energetic shift around my fulcrum, both locally and in other parts of the body which are related to the involved joint. I hold this balance until I *see* the signs of the "working state" or until some other signal guides me to release my hold.

When I remove my hands, usually in the range of ten to thirty seconds, and reevaluate the function of the original part, there usually is improvement of the joint function. This represents an energetic shift, and the client will have the feeling that "something has improved."

When I establish a fulcrum and hold it in a state of nonchange, the body itself changes around my stationary point. In a system which is always in motion, the more stationary we become in one place, the greater our leverage for movement on another part of the system. The shifts which occur in adaptation to the fulcrum are initiated from the body's own energetic, psychologic, and physiologic mechanisms. They occur internally and naturally rather than being initiated externally. In my experience, these shifts last longer and have farther reaching effects for the person than changes brought about by direct change through manipulation per se.

Observable Therapeutic Response

With the foregoing definitions and working principles in mind, let us now look at the responses of the experiencer. There are major and minor observable signs which are indicative of the working state. It is important to point out that no one sign is "supposed" to occur in response to an energetic stimulation. There are a number of possibilities, and our task is merely to witness what happens. We never force any specific reaction.

The major landmarks include the eyes, the breath, and voice vitality. The minor landmarks include changes of color, sound, odor, body response and movement, and environmental shifts.

Major Therapeutic Response: The Eyes

The first of the major guidelines concerns changes in the eyes and eyelids. I prefer that a client lie on his or her back for energy balancing work, partially so I can observe the response. One person may close the eyes and another may leave them open. Since we are witnessing the person's natural responses, we do not ask that the eyes be either open or closed. Let the person do what is most natural and comfortable, and let us learn to read either response.

Assume that the person is lying on the table with eyes open. Until the subject is relaxed, most information gained is not energetically significant. He or she may be looking directly at the therapist or at objects in the room or at nothing particular. As the person becomes more comfortable the eyes will soften and perhaps begin to wander in an abstracted way. In a few moments they will often close.

Closed Eye Signs

The major sign of the working state, with eyes closed, is rapid eye motion (REM). As the name implies, REM is manifest as a rapid eyelid flutter. If you are not acquainted with what a REM looks like, have someone close his or her eyes and, keeping them closed, look up toward the forehead, A fine flutter of the eyelids will develop.

This is a REM flutter.

REMs are indicative of an altered state of consciousness, and occur naturally during our sleep and while we dream. Although studies indicate that alpha brain waves are associated with REMs, my experience is that not all REM states indicate alpha brain wave activity. REMs occur frequently in energy work studies where EEGs failed to show any increase of alpha brain wave activity.

In energy work the length of the REM is not directly related to the depth and duration of the stimulus. In acupuncture when the needle contacts the acupuncture point the person often lapses into spontaneous REMs. If the acupuncture needle is left in place for fifteen or twenty minutes a person will drift in and out of the REM state. However, if the point is stimulated for one or two seconds, activating the REM process, and then the needle is withdrawn, the person may continue to move in and out of the REM state for several minutes if he or she rests undisturbed on the table. On other occasions, the REMs may stop immediately after the needle is removed. Responses may or may not continue beyond the end of the stimulus.

When a person is lying with the eyes closed, movement of the eyeball from side to side beneath the lid may occur. This does not constitute a REM, nor is it the working state. The subject is wandering within ordinary consciousness. As a subject gives over to relaxation, this will subside.

Open Eye Signs

If the person's eyes remain open after we make an essential connection, three common responses are seen:

First is the "fixed stare." The eyes may have been wandering or softly looking at the ceiling when they seem suddenly to stop and be riveted on some specific point. This fixed stare may last as few as several seconds or as long as several minutes before the eyes soften again and resume a wandering pattern. This is like a soldier moving from "at ease" to "attention" and back again.

Second is the "glazed look" of the eyeball. The eyes may have been glistening and alert, but suddenly when the energy body is contacted they become glazed, dull, empty, and flat. It is as if the consciousness has been withdrawn from the eyes and "nobody is at home." This glazed, blank expression can occur repeatedly throughout a session and may last from a split second to minutes. If at the end of the session a person continues to manifest glazed eyes we can assume he or she is still in an altered state of awareness. Left alone, this state will gradually subside in the course of normal activities. However, if the person needs to be fully alert, perhaps to drive a car, normal consciousness can be easily induced by directing the subject to perform a purposeful action. This can be anything from walking across the room to carrying on a conversation.

The last common response is "sudden eye closure." In this case the person is resting and the eyes are soft, perhaps looking around the room aimlessly. The eyelids are performing normal blinking. As we contact the energy through our stimulus, the eyelids may suddenly "slam shut" as through someone had pulled a shade down. The eyelids will stay closed for perhaps five to ten seconds and then will suddenly open as if the shade had flipped up. The person will return to normal blinking. On receipt of another stimulus there may be another sudden closure followed by a sudden opening, and then the normal blinking. This movement of the eyelids is very obvious and distinct from the normal blinking mechanism.

In energy work, change of the size of the pupil itself is not a guide to the working state. The pupils stay the same size despite the essential connection, and do not alter as other eye signs occur.

Major Therapeutic Response: Breath Patterns

The second major criterion to witness in energy balancing work is the breath pattern. Breathing is the one function of the body which is directly responsive to both our voluntary and autonomic nervous systems, and it is a key bridge between the conscious and unconscious. The breath is a primary source of our energy and vibration. In energy work, the response of the breath pattern is a direct signal of energetic shifts in the body.

During an energy therapy session I want to monitor the breath, and if an individual consciously manipulates the breathing in a manner he or she feels is "intellectually correct," such as "breathing into" an area of discomfort or "blowing off tension," I will specifically ask the individual to breathe normally. I do not say that I plan to observe the breath pattern since this would make the client self-conscious, thereby disturbing the spontaneous reactions. My suggestion is simply to breathe normally, relax, and enjoy the session.

Several specific terms are used to describe the breathing pattern:

"Hyperpnea" denotes a "large breath"; *hyper* means excess or exaggerated and *pnea* means breath.

"Hypopnea" denotes a small or shallow breath; *hypo* means lower.

"Relative apnea" indicates a shallow breath, and is used interchangeably with hypopnea.

"Apnea" literally means without breath. Through clothing it often looks as if the person isn't breathing and so the term apnea is used to describe the pattern. In actuality, hypopnea is usually more accurate.

In the breath patterns, the shallow breaths usually occur in a series and both the amplitude and the rate of respiration are lessened. The hyperpneas, however, tend to occur singulary and are related to amplitude only.

The Working Breath Cycle

With the subject lying on his or her back, our witness consciousness scans and observes. As the person relaxes and settles into the session, the breathing normally becomes rhythmic, slightly slower, and shallower. Until a relaxed breath pattern arrives, little significant information can be noted. Once the normal breath pattern is operative, we become alert to small changes. The "working breath cycle" is an *involuntary* response and most typically consists of a cycle of relative apnea, followed by one hyperpnea. The hypopnea cycle is of a variable duration, perhaps ten to thirty seconds, followed by one large inhalation, which is then followed by the normal respiratory pattern.

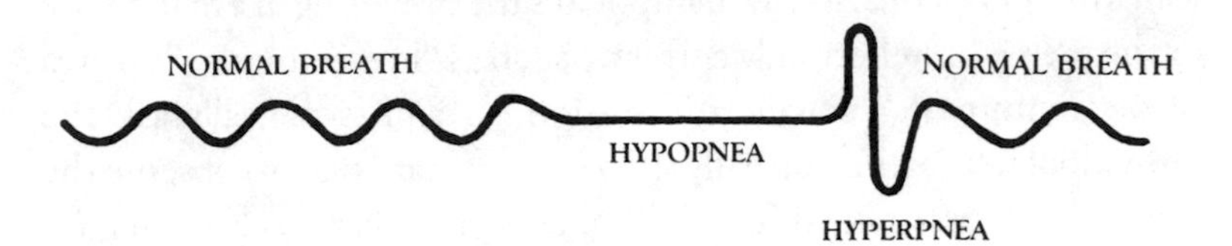

If the normal breathing pattern of the person is already quite slow and shallow, we may not perceive a subtle relative apneic phase through clothing, and may only be aware of the hyperpnea at the end of the cycle. In other cases, in a very light working state, the close of the cycle may only be a sniff. I consider a "freestanding" hyperpnea or sniff as indicating the closure of the working cycle and assume my witness missed the hypopneic phase.

Relations of Breath Pattern to Stimulus

The occurrence of the breath pattern in relation to the applied stimulus and essential touch varies. Most frequently one, two, or three normal breaths are required after the stimulation before the hypopneic phase begins.

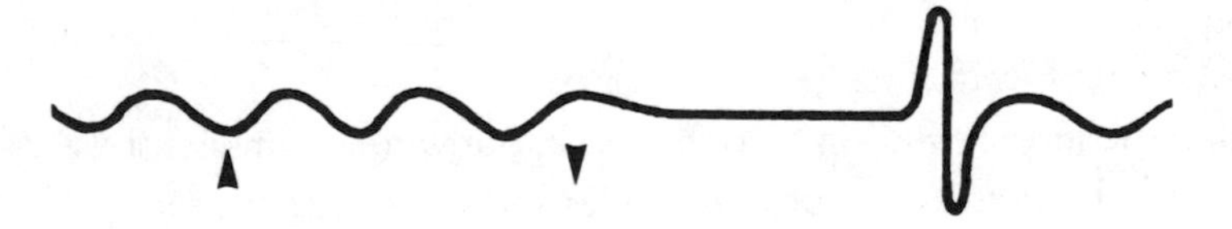

▲ STIMULUS APPLIED
▼ STIMULUS REMOVED

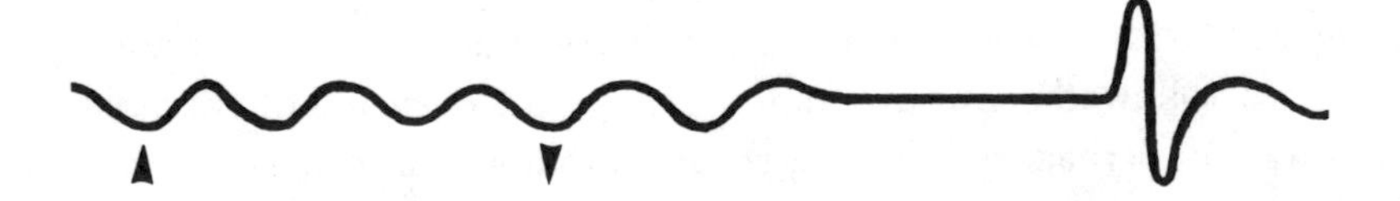

It is also possible to have a response develop over a succession of stimuli. The first stimulus may cause a slight apnea, but no hyperpnea closure. The second and third stimuli produce a longer apnea, and finally the fourth or fifth stimulus will produce the typical response. These repeated stimuli may be the same fulcrum repeated, or may be a linear progression of fulcrums or acupuncture points in a treatment session.

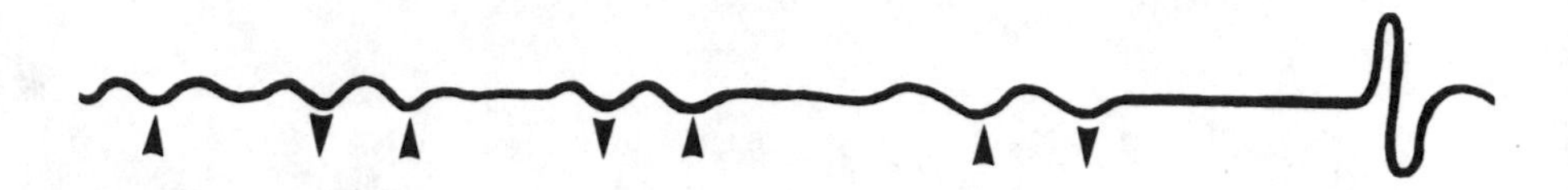

▲ STIMULUS APPLIED

▼ STIMULUS REMOVED

Some people repeatedly go from shallow breath back into the normal breath pattern without having a concluding hyperpnea or sniff. With these people I will not use the breath to monitor the energetic response because I do not consider this a full breath cycle. Rather, I will look for clearer signals from other parts of the body.

▲ STIMULUS APPLIED

▼ STIMULUS REMOVED

The length of time we maintain the stimulus will vary, depending on the relationship of the stimulus to the breath response. If the hypopneic phase begins to develop shortly after we apply stimulation, we may elect to hold the stimulus throughout the cycle. The total time lapse may be fifteen to thirty seconds.

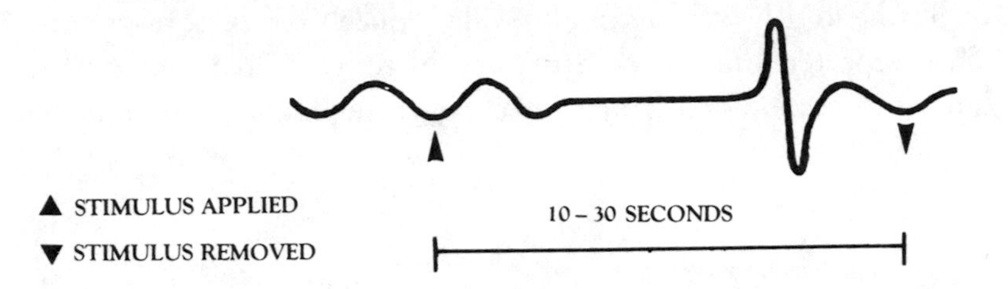

If the hypopneic phase requires a little longer to develop, we may choose to remove the stimulus as it begins, and then wait for the completion of the cycle before we move on.

Some people have little or no breath manifestation until the treatment has concluded. Often as the person is resting at the end of the session he or she will then drop into a deep and profound apnea stage. If this occurs, I wait for the concluding hyperpnea before considering the session complete. If the apnea seems too prolonged it can be interrupted by a gentle additional stimulus, such as a touch to the leg or foot, or by asking the person to take a breath. An involuntary hyperpnea usually follows.

At the end of a typical treatment there will be a few moments of deep relaxation and altered awareness with repeated REMs and shallow breathing. The signal for the actual completion of the session is a special breath, movement sequence. Typically the person will have a period of hypopnea and with one hyperpnea, followed by a throat reflex of swallowing, a facial grimace, and an eye reflex of blinking, at which time the eyes will open, clear and sparkling.

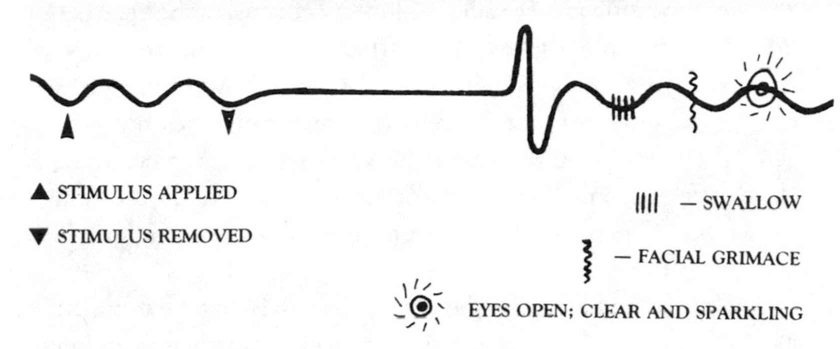

Breath Pattern: Rationale

The working breath cycle — the hypopnea followed by the hyperpnea — is an involuntary response to an energetic stimulation. Our stimulation overrides the usual breath control mechanism, and the depth and length that we hold the fulcrum influences the length of the relative apneic phase.

According to Western physiology, breathing is responsive to both the autonomic and voluntary nervous systems.

In addition, Traditional Chinese Medicine discusses the *ch'i*, or energy contained within the air, which enters the body via the breath. Our requirement of ch'i from this source, and its inherent vibration, would appear to be a third factor involved in the regulation of normal breathing. If there is a deficiency of vibration, the breath may increase; if an excess, breathing may become more shallow, depending on the voluntary and metabolic (autonomic) requirements of that moment.

A variety of stimuli can induce a shallow breath. For instance, one inhalation through the nose strong enough to be audible and to activate the venturi mechanism (see chapter 6) will lead to relative apnea. A body contact of an essential nature — traction on the legs, a fulcrum on the shoulder girdle or needle stimulation to an acupuncture point — will frequently induce a shallow breath.

The exact mechanism of this involuntary breath response, from a Western physiological viewpoint, is curious. A two- or three-second acupuncture needle stimulation does not cause significant behavioral change in the individual to affect voluntary control of the breath; nor does it affect the blood gases. The fact that autonomic functions (pupil size, skin moisture or temperature, heart rate, bowel function) are unchanged indicates that the needle stimulation does not have a general effect on the autonomic nervous system. Yet breathing *is* clearly affected, and this response occurs regardless of the location of the acupuncture point, thus discounting a direct nerve reflex which affects breathing.

The *energetic rationale* for the shallow breath is that the stimulation itself supplies or releases energy or vibration, relieving for a moment the necessity for the breath to supply it. The longer and more deeply we apply the stimulation, the more vibration is released and the longer the relative apnea. However, given time, either an additional need for ch'i or an alteration in the blood gases stimulates the hyperpnea response and balances the body.

Major Therapeutic Response: Voice Vitality

The third major observable energetic response is the vitality of the person's voice. Whereas this is not truly a response we can observe as we can the REMs and the breath, it is an easily accessible gauge of the general level of fullness or depletion of the subtle body. The *quality and the vitality of vibration* in the voice is involuntary and is of major significance. Periodically during an energy balancing session I will ask the person how he or she is and listen for both the words and the vitality of the response. Of the two, the latter is the most important. "I'm OK" spoken in flat, dull, barely audible tones means that energetically he or she is not OK. The flat quality is a sign of energy depletion and indicates that the energy session should move faster, be staccato, and that the person should be closely monitored for any further signs of depletion. The response to "how are you" may be a head nod, and again, it is the vitality or lack of vitality of the nod that is significant rather than the OK designation.

Minor Therapeutic Responses

Beyond the major signs of the eyes, breath, and voice vitality, are a number of less significant signs. They do not specifically indicate the working state itself, but that the body is responding or has responded to an energetic shift. They are often transient phenomena, not particulary helpful in determining how long or how deeply each fulcrum should be held, but in conjunction with the major signs, they complete our picture of the individual's internal process of response to our energetic interaction.

Borborisms

One minor sign of the person responding to energy work is borborismus, a rumbling or gurgling of the bowel. It is such a common reaction to stimulation that we take it as a sign of a shift in the subtle body. Of course, borborismus can be caused by something the person ate before coming for a treatment, or may represent hunger. When it occurs in exact and repeated correspondence with an energetic stimulus, we consider it most likely represents a shift in the patient's energy system.

In our culture we are conditioned to feel somewhat embarrassed with any bowel noise, and this embarrassment may lead to inhibition of energy movement in the body. When I hear a borborismus, I take a moment to reassure the person that this is a good sign, to offset any embarrassment, and lessen the likelihood of the patient inhibiting the energy flow.

Odor

An oft-neglected or undiscussed phenomenon is that of abrupt change of body odor. It is not uncommon for people who smoke or have smoked cigarettes to suddenly emit a strong tobacco odor during the balancing of the energy system, even if they have not smoked for a number of years. This is also true of other substances such as garlic or alcohol, though neither has been recently ingested. A person may even emit the familiar odor of ether, residual of some long past anaesthesia. Odors related to past experience are usually a one-time occurrence, and are indicative of the release of an entrapped vibration from the body.

Color

For people who see auras and understand their configurations, color signs surrounding or on the body may represent a major rather than a minor guideline. This is also true of people who read color in reference to the five elements of Chinese medicine. Colors may also abruptly change in the same way odors do. I recall one patient from whose face an orange color, almost like syrup, began to rise and pour. I have never understood its exact significance but the person felt fundamentally and significantly better after the session.

In Traditional Chinese Medicine, sound, odor, and color changes have a special significance. Each of the five elements has a number of correspondences (see diagram) which commonly fluctuate during any Traditional Chinese Medicine acupuncture or energy balancing session. These changes give insight into the elemental response of the person, to meridian pathways stimulated, or to underlying emotional release.

CORRESPONDENCES OF THE FIVE ELEMENTS

	METAL	WATER	WOOD	FIRE	EARTH
Emotion	grief	fear	anger	joy	sympathy
Color	white	blue /black	green	red	yellow
Odor	rotten	putrid	rancid	scorched	fragrant
Sound	weeping	groaning	shouting	laughing	singing

Meridians

Acupuncture meridians can act as minor indicators of energy response. If we intentionally or inadvertently stimulate a meridian, we may see the body responding at distant points along the pathway. For instance, it is not uncommon to be working on the outside of the foot and have the person brush his hand over his forehead or rub his eyes in a nonchalant manner. If we know that the bladder meridian begins at the inner corner of the eye, comes up over the forehead, and then moves down the back and leg to the outside of the foot, it makes perfect sense that this stimulation caused a reaction on the forehead or eye. If we didn't know the anatomy of this particular meridian pathway, the innocent eye-brushing motion would have escaped our attention. The greater our knowledge of the meridian pathways, and of energy anatomy in general, the more we understand correlations of stimulus and response.

Shelving

In this phenomenon we perceive planes of the body moving in opposite directions. I think of geological formations, like parallel lines of shale on the exposed surface of a hillside, which frequently show signs of having shifted from an original position. When I see shelving occurring in the body, what I mentally envision happening is one energetic level shifting or gliding on another. It is common to observe this in the chest and abdomen and it may occur any number of times during a session, each shelving experience lasting several seconds. This is a subliminal body response; most people are unaware of any bodily sensation; a few report a mild "shaking." Shelving represents a reorganization and integration of the subtle and physical body.

Movement

Sometimes during an energy balancing session, body jerks or "physical kriyas" will occur. In therapeutic energy work, major kriyas rarely occur. As I have already discussed, minor twitches and jerking of various parts of the body are not uncommon in people who have done meditative practices. If necessary, the intensity of kriyas can be reduced if we engage the body more on the physical and less on the energetic plane by making more definite physical contact. Not all jerking or twitching motions are kriyas. Some may be caused by neuromuscular reflexes or through activation of meridian systems. It is not always possible to distinguish a small kriya from other types of muscular response.

Serenity

Most body therapy sessions lead to a state of relaxation. When a person has experienced an essential connection, he or she experiences a response beyond relaxation— one of acceptance, internal peace, and serenity. A concurrent angelic expression is often seen. This depth of response is a sign of an energetic connection.

Environmental Shifts

A peculiar minor sign sometimes occurs that is experienced as an abrupt alteration of the room's atmosphere. The room seems to suddenly become dense and still. This is a normal result of two energy fields meeting in an essential way. The calm which occurs is almost palpable and is experienced by everyone in the room, not just by the two people involved in the session. I am reminded of metal filings which line up as a magnet is passed nearby.

Areas of Caution in Energy Balancing Work

Imposition

Energy work is relatively safe, but as in all therapy systems there are potential hazards. The first word of caution is not to let our expectations get in the way and "force" the person's subtle body to respond in a specific way. Each person will have his or her own way of responding to energetic stimulation, and it is our job to observe what this is. If we attempt to create a breath cycle or a REM when there is no inclination for it to occur of its own accord, we are imposing our will and energy on the person. If we override the natural response, we can actually create imbalance and chaos.

Imprinting

Another problem area is negative or disharmonic imprinting. This is especially true if the individual is in an altered or heightened state of awareness, when we are working beneath his or her level of conscious control, or are on the growing edge of his or her experience. We must be acutely aware of words and gestures in these therapeutic situations.

While a person is exhibiting breath cycles or other signs of "working," the standard defense mechanisms are less active, and vibrations that we induce may imprint deeply in the body /mind /spirit. The vibration can be instilled through touch, words, and thoughts (see chapter 5, Red Flags).

Depletion

In energetic work energy depletion may become a problem, particulary if we override the normal respirator mechanisms for too long and induce a state of oxygen deprivation.

Early in my teaching I was giving Zero Balancing treatment to a young woman. It was late in the day on a hot summer afternoon. The classroom was stuffy and everyone was tired and low on energy.

Signs of energetic movement came easily as I began to work on the young woman; the REMs occurred as did relative apneas and hyperpneas, providing a good demonstration of these particular signs. Then, three-quarters of the way through the session, I noticed that she was having prolonged hypopneas and looked extremely relaxed and serene. I leaned over and asked her how she was doing. To my surprise, she did not respond. I inquired more loudly, and still there was no response. Suddenly I became alarmed. Observing her more closely, I saw that her appearance resembled porcelain; she was pale and when I felt her forehead it was cold and clammy. I immediately went to the foot of the table and stimulated her through her feet and legs. As she began to respond I asked her how she was feeling. She answered, "I'm fine," but her voice had no vitality or animation. As soon as I let go of her ankles she dropped back into a nonresponsive state with REMs and very shallow respirations. I continued to stimulate her, until her color returned, her voice had vitality, and she was fully alert.

I later asked her to describe her experience with the treatment. She said that it had been "a lovely session," that she felt fine, and had "felt far out of my body." Even though she had heard my voice when I spoke to her, she did not respond because, as she said, "I didn't want to come back."

Her last statement frightened me because, from an objective viewpoint, she had not been fine. In retrospect I realized that the repeated, excessively long periods of shallow respiration had induced a state of low oxygenation and central nervous system depression. Her pale, colorless appearance, cold sweat, and lack of vital response was reminiscent of people I had seen in hospital emergency rooms suffering from primary shock. I have often wondered if she might have developed cardiac arrest had we continued in the direction we were moving. This session alerted me to the possibility of causing harm through energy work, and resulted in my establishing specific guidelines for monitoring treatments and enumerating early danger signals.

Danger Signals of Depletion

Danger signals which alert us to depletion are: general lack of vitality; paleness; sweating, especially cold sweat; stuffy nose; yawning; languidness; and /or cold extremities.

General Vitality

This can most easily be monitored through the voice, by asking questions and listening to the *timing* and *tone* of each response. If the person responds *immediately,* he or she is in the here and now; if there is a long delay, he or she may be in an altered state of consciousness. If the response is crisp and alert, the energy level is good; if the answer sounds feeble or lifeless, it indicates possible depletion, regardless of the sense of the words the person speaks.

Paleness

As a person relaxes, the color normally changes, becoming less pink or red. The paleness from decreased activity should be distinguished from the pallor of depletion. Pallor, pastiness, greyish or greyish blue skin color, may indicate oxygen and/or ch'i depletion, especially when associated with cold sweat, and with prolonged shallow respiration.

Cold Sweat

In energy work, cold sweat or dampness may be an early sign of depletion, especially if associated with pallor. It is more frequently first seen in the forehead or extremities.

Stuffy Nose

This may represent the body's formation of venturi tubes (see chapter 6) to offset energy depletion.

Yawning

A "sigh" is evidence of relaxation. A "sniff" often signals the end of a working breath cycle. A "yawn" is a venturi tube more powerful than the stuffy nose and should be interpreted as a sign of depletion until proven otherwise.

Languidness

Another expression of lack of vitality is any postural configuration indicating languidness. This is not to be confused with the increasing state of relaxation a person normally develops during a treatment session, where the breathing becomes lower and shallower, muscle tension falls away, and the person more or less sinks into the table. With languidenss, a person's head may roll to one side or the other, or an arm may listlessly hang off the table. The person seems quite "absent." If there is any doubt about vitality, ask the person how he or she is doing.

Cold Extremities

Cold extremities are significant if a person becomes cold and sweaty during a treatment session. Many people have cold, sweaty palms or feet from the outset, which makes this sign less reliable.

The important thing to realize is that *despite early energy depletion a person may report feeling well.* The early state of depletion is not unpleasant and may be associated with feelings of peace, tranquility, and altered states of consciousness. However, altered states achieved through depletion or fatigue are not healthy. They may deplete the energy body and result in ongoing fatigue or depression; they may deplete the physical body of oxygen and lead to deprivation. Any one danger sign of depleted ch'i or oxygen may alone not be significant, but even one of them should alert us to potential problems and cause us to monitor the person more closely. If danger signs come as a group there is a higher likelihood that depletion is occurring.

Treatment of Depletion

If, during hands-on treatment, we suspect that we may be depleting a person, it is critical that we take control. To offset depletion, move faster, be more physical than energetic, and stimulate the person with the hands. Disallow long apneas and repeated REMs. Make the fulcrums briefer, yet firmer; engage the subject in conversation; ask him or her to take several deep breaths. With a change of pace we should see signs of depletion disappear. If not, close the treatment in relatively short order and stay present. At the close of the session, have the person get up rather than remain relaxing on the table and possibly draining further. If the client is the least bit chilly or thirsty, a warm sweater or cup of hot tea can be helpful. If we do elect to leave the person on the table a few moments, he or she should lie on one side with the knees slightly drawn up to contain the energy field.

Factors Favoring Depletion

Certain people are more likely to develop depletion than others. The most common combination of factors favoring depletion is found in the person who is a vegetarian, a meditator, and/or a person who has a past history of drug experience. Not all people with this history will develop problems, but be alert to this group as a whole, particulary to the person who naturally has a pale complexion; a thin, asthenic body build; and a soft voice.

People who are vegetarians have a finer energy field vibration that people who are not. People who are fruitarians have a finer field than vegetarians. With these finer vibrations energy moves faster, and does not seem as "attached" to the physical body as in people with broader dietary habits.

People who meditate a great deal or who have done so in the past have activated their energy systems, and have cleared themselves of a number of obstructions so that their energy flows more quickly. They are also accustomed to the feeling of "running on ch'i" itself and frequently gravitate toward altered states or out-of-body experiences.

People who have used hallucinatory and social drugs are familiar with altered states and frequently have had out-of-body experiences. These people understand astral travel, and those who enjoy the feeling of disembodiment, given a stimulus, are inclined to move in that direction. The less grounded a person is the greater the tendency to "space out," especially when we are there to act as the grounding force. If this is carried too far, it can deplete the energy. The object of energy work is to balance a person, not to provide an experience.

One major clue to whether a person might potentially deplete is how quickly he or she responds to an energetic stimulus. A person who lies down and immediately goes into REMs or whose breathing quickly lapses into relative apnea is a person who moves readily into altered states of consciousness. With such a person I recommend working at a more staccato pace for a shorter period of time.

A number of years ago a man visited my workshop and asked to experience hands-on energy work. This was early in my career before I had comprehended the potential magnitude of energetic work and, without taking an adequate history, I consented to work with him. He stretched out on the table and I put my hand on his legs to orient to him with a half-moon fulcrum. The very moment I touched him he went into REMs and shallow respirations. I asked him how he was and already his voice had lost significant vitality. Obviously it was not appropriate to continue any sort of energy treatment, so I began to stimulate the return of ordinary consciousness. When he seemed alert and present, I removed my hands, whereupon he dropped back into REMs, hypopnea, and nonresponsiveness. It took me over fifteen minutes just to get him stable enough so that I could take my hands away and have him run on his own power. All of this happened before I had done anything other than to lift his legs to apply traction. Later I queried him on his history. It turned out he had been taking LSD daily for the past ten days. His energy fields were so distorted and loose that just by touching him briefly in an essential way the fields collapsed. Do not do energy work on people who are on heavy drugs, and be careful of those who have long, complicated drug histories. Their responses may be very rapid, erratic, and different from what one customarily encounters.

Each of us reacts differently to an alteration of our energy state. Some people under high stress or in high vibratory fields react by becoming more grounded, more exact, more firm and rooted. Other persons under stress let go of or lose their grounding, space out, and escape into a fantasy world.

Often, the ideal energy treatment is to create a higher energy field and then guide the person's response in the *opposite direction* from that to which the person is accustomed. The person who habitually becomes more grounded is encouraged to expand the body energy toward an altered state experience, to embrace lightness and freedom, and to experience sensations of elongating, compacting, or floating. As we see REMs, apneas, and indications of an altered state, we might prolong the fulcrums.

With the person who is so used to altered states that whenever the eyes are closed spontaneous REMs occur, the object is to contain the energy within the figure eight flows and prevent out-of-body experiences. The sensation may not "feel" as pleasant, will not be "spacey" or "electric," but will in truth be of greater service. By conserving the high vibrations within the physical body and its internal energy field, strength, vitality, and groundedness will be augmented, and the person will begin to develop alternative ways of dealing with stress.

Conclusion

A person cannot not react and the process of witnessing the response to an energy balancing session is informative. Knowing maps of possible inner journeys and involuntary responses helps objectify and make tangible a largely subjective skill. It also provides us insights into a person's energy nature, and allows us to participate safely, effectively, and fully in the energy balancing process.

5
Bridges of Caution

Exercise your art solely for the cure of your patient.
— Hippocratic Oath

"Do no harm" is one of the basic tenets of the healing professions, both ancient and modern. On casual observation "do no harm" seems to be a simple enough principle, but on closer examination it becomes more complex. In this chapter, issues will be considered which help the practitioner to "exercise your art solely for the cure of the patient." The areas center on diagnosis of illness, communication in the therapeutic setting, and creating a healing perspective.

Diagnosis of Illness

In many cases the cause of a problem is clear, and the patient can readily decide what course of therapy to follow. In other cases the nature, extent, or diagnosis of an illness has not been established and the direction of further care is difficult to determine. In my opinion, if there is ever a serious question about where to begin, a *health evaluation* in the medical model needs to prevail. To "do no harm" begins with making certain that no gross pathology is overlooked. Once a medical evaluation has been completed and information about the pathology becomes known, the direction of further care is more easily decided.

Red Flags

A number of situations, or "Red Flags," alert one to the importance of seeking a conventional medical opinion. Their order is arbitrary, not suggesting relative importance. These guidelines are not meant to be all inclusive.

Unexplained Weight Change

A change in body weight indicates a significant shift in the homeostasis of the body, and the reason for this shift must be ascertained. Unexplained weight loss is usually of greater concern than unexplained weight gain. The causes of weight loss include diabetes, cancer, tuberculosis (on the rise again), acquired immunity deficiency syndrome (AIDS), endocrine problems, chronic infectious disease, cirrhosis of the liver, psychosomatic problems, and mental stress. A family history is helpful, because many problems are recurrent in families. Of particular concern is weight loss when associated with other symptoms like abnormal bleeding, changed bowel habits, night sweats, unexplained fatigue, and so on.

Unexplained weight loss in a person with a cancer history *demands* an evaluation. Many people recover totally from cancer. If a cancer does return, its return is most frequent within the first five years after treatment. If no signs of a recurrence appear during that time, the chances of relapse are so greatly reduced that a five-year survival is considered a cure. Unfortunately, however, cancer can return at any time, and so even the five-year-cured person must remain alert.

People with a cancer history carry with them the deep fear of its possible return. Whenever exploring the possibility of recurrence with someone, high level communication skills are needed. Any small squeak or rattle in the body can set off an alarm reaction. Some people are so fearful that in the face of significant symptoms they *do not* go to their physician specifically because they are afraid of a diagnosis of the recurrence of cancer. They may go to an alternative health care provider hoping for a more benign diagnosis. The medical examination is important for at least two reasons: first, if the problem has recurred, treatment alternatives can be evaluated and begun without losing valuable time; and if the problem has not recurred, that very information will help nullify the fear, which itself may have brought on stress and poor health. The wait-and-see attitude for weight loss in someone with a cancer history is untenable.

Unexplained weight gain is less frequent than weight loss. It could represent kidney, heart, or endocrine dysfunction. As with weight loss, the cause must be determined.

Abnormal Bleeding from Any Body Orifice

This is one of the cardinal signs in medicine which calls for investigation. Obviously the location of the bleeding will determine the urgency and type of examination. Frequent causes include tumor (malignant or benign), infections, ulcer, inflammatory process, hormonal imbalances and trauma.

Change in Body Functions

A significant change in any body function is a "red flag." Of particular importance is the change in bowel habits of a person (especially a man) over forty; bowel cancer is not uncommon.

Physical Change

There may be physical changes in the body with no change of function. Primary causes for concern are any new mass or tumor, especially in the breast, any old tumor which changes in any way, any change in a pigmented area or mole. Other examples include swelling sores that do not heal, persistent rashes, and migratory joint pain.

In the course of health care, stay aware that anyone might have a silent problem totally unrelated to the reason for consultation. In one three month period during energy balancing sessions I "accidentally" discovered two fibroid tumors, a kidney cyst, and an abdominal aneurism. In the latter case the gentleman was on an operating table within six hours after he was referred to a medical specialist. Remember that anyone can have a problem of which he is unaware. Staying alert to *anything* out of the ordinary may literally save someone's life.

Trauma

This category covers many situations, and is particularly important because we are all solicited for help and advice by friends, family, and acquaintances who have just injured themselves. Alternative health care practitioners particularly must be careful when dealing with people who come for pain relief from a very recent injury; the questions practitioners must ask themselves include "how badly is the person hurt and is the problem beyond my technical skill and legal license?" Certainly not every trauma needs to be seen by a doctor, but if in doubt, do not hesitate to refer the person.

It is *absolutely wrong* to say that if someone can use an injured part it is not broken. In the course of my own practice, I have seen individuals walk into my office with a broken ankle, a broken hip, a broken pelvis, a fractured vertebra (quite common), and even with a broken neck. The fact that a person can move or walk on a part does *not* mean that there is no fracture. Whenever a person has had a trauma to the skeletal system, the possibility of a fracture exists. The probability is related to the severity of the injury, the amount of pain suffered, the age and health of the individual, the appearance and tenderness of the injured area, and the length of time since the accident occurred.

Fractures may be stable or unstable; some fractures are significant, others are annoying but basically not an important problem. Immediate skillful care is imperative for some fractures, while others may be ignored or simply taped or isolated for a period. Final diagnosis of fractures rests on X-ray findings or on the newer types of evaluation of the skeletal system. Well-taken X-rays are quite reliable, but some fractures do not show on initial films; the fracture only becomes visible three or four weeks afterwards, when bone absorption in the healing process makes the fracture more evident.

Several common trauma situations need special comment. The

first of these is a fall, in which one lands solidly on one's buttocks. The force from the fall goes directly up into the spine and because of the normal curves of the back, if the energy impact is too great, the vertebrae will buckle under the impact rather than conduct the forces around the curves and up the vertebral column. I treated one man who was driving fast in a jeep which hit a chuckhole. The impact caused a compression fracture of the first lumbar vertebra. Variations of this "pratfall" occur anytime a direct sudden impact occurs vertically through the body, including blows directly on top of the shoulders or head.

Simple compression fractures of bones in the back are common. Fortunately most of them are relatively stable, do not shift significantly from the vertical line, and do not create much of an immediate problem other than pain. However, post-traumatic arthritis may occur, and if vertebral height is significantly reduced, over the years body posture is affected, with the result of forward stooping.

Displaced or unstable vertebral fractures are totally different, because of the possibility of spinal cord injuries. These problems are severe and require skilled medical care. One major issue with these injuries is not to compound the problem by excessive movement of the spine just after the injury. Landing on the head or neck as when falling off a bike, diving into shallow water, or bodysurfing in shallow water, can result in potentially disastrous cervical fractures.

Pathologic Fractures

A special group of fractures known as "pathologic fractures" occur because of underlying bony pathology. Bone itself has no pain fibers, and it is only when the bone covering (the periostium) is compromised that "bone pain" occurs. This means a person can have severe bony destruction without being aware of it. A pathologic fracture may actually be the first sign that there is an underlying problem. A seemingly mild traumatic incident can cause a fracture. Women after menopause may develop osteoporosis, or "decalcification" of the bone, resulting from hormonal changes. Bones which decalcify lose strength and fracture easily. A fall for a woman of sixty-five who has osteoporosis may result in a major fracture while the same fall for a woman of thirty may result in nothing more than a bruise.

Other conditions which might contribute to bone weakening include prolonged cortisone therapy (causing demineralization), benign bony cysts or cancer (weakening of the architecture), aging (demineralization, diminished bone flexibility), and bone disease per se (Paget's disease, Tuberculosis).

Another group of unsuspected fractures is the stress fracture. The "march fracture" was documented in armed services when soldiers developed fractures of the long bones of the feet from marching excessive distances. We see march fractures in joggers and competitive walkers. Often stress fractures occur in hips of elderly people. Many times a person will turn or move, hear a snap in his hip, and fall to the ground. The fracture actually happened as a result of the movement and precipitated the fall instead of being caused by the fall itself.

Sometimes complaints of bone or joint pain have other causes. For example, a number of years ago, a woman came to me complaining of moderately severe hip pain, which she had been suffering for about a month. The significant historical fact was that she had had breast cancer four years earlier. Upon hearing this, a red flag went up in my mind. Yet one week prior to consulting me she had seen an orthopedist whose X-rays showed no pathology. She had come to me for alternative therapy, not wanting to take pain medication. My evaluation showed a significant energetic imbalance in the hip. After three treatments, however, the patient reported no improvement. In view of the continuing pain, I referred her to her orthopedist again. He took new X-rays which showed metastatic cancer. In just a two-week period the X-rays had gone from normal to abnormal.

This case illustrates several issues. When complaints persist despite recent tests, retesting may be necessary, and constitutes good medical practice. Second, if any therapy does not bring improvement within a reasonable period of time, it should be acknowledged as being ineffective. Third, the presence of a number of mental red flags (a history of cancer plus unexplained pain) quickly alerts a practitioner to the proper course of action.

Unexplained Fevers

This is another cardinal sign for a diagnostic workup. Cancers of all sorts, primary or metastatic, may first manifest as a fever. Connective tissue disease (rheumatic fever, rheumatoid arthritis, lupus erythemetosis), infection (AIDS, hepatitis, malaria), drug reactions, serum sickness, and blood clots are all possible causes of otherwise "unexplained" fever.

Inflammatory Processes

The signs of inflammation are redness, heat, swelling, and pain. Inflammation can occur with infection (boils, gonorrheal arthritis) or without (gouty arthritis, Reiter's syndrome, tendonitis, sprains, fractures). The occurrence of these four signs calls for a medical differential diagnosis.

Infectious Processes

Severe or recurrent infectious processes require medical attention. A superficial infection such as a cut or sore anywhere on the body which develops red streaks from the primary site of the infection is indicative of spreading infection. Infections which don't heal may be a sign of an underlying pathology such as diabetes. Ongoing infections, such as candida albicans (monilia), may cause general body symptoms. Gonorrhea may lead to infectious arthritis. Tuberculosis can lead to any number of body changes including weight loss, fatigue, coughing, and general debility.

Medical Drugs

A number of issues concern prescribed medication. Persons in alternative therapies do well to have knowledge of the common drugs, but of course, do not become involved in their management. Prescribing, altering, or stopping medical drugs is in the province of the medical community. Drugs are concentrated and potent, and may instigate *side effects* (headaches with nitroglycerine, osteoporosis with cortisone), *drug reactions* (nausea with codeine), or *drug allergies* (rash with penicillin). If it seems possible that a drug is causing a problem, refer the person to the prescribing physician or to someone in the medical community. With certain medications, drug dosages must be changed slowly, because abrupt changes can be problematic or dangerous.

So many people are on prescription drugs that it is helpful for alternative health care providers to have ready sources of information. This support system might, at least, include a doctor, a pharmacist, and a copy of the *Physician's Desk Reference* (PDR).

Pain

Pain may arise from any level within a person: physical, mental (and emotional), or spiritual. Energetically, pain is caused by movement being blocked. The pain itself may be diverted or alleviated with medication or through an alternative therapy, but do not overlook the underlying cause. Pain serves as a warning signal and to merely stop it, without finding its cause, is contrary to good sense.

The Ill-looking Person

The more ill a person, the more urgent the need for a medical opinion. Usually energetic problems do not make a person look as ill as do physical disturbances of body functions.

Complaints Outside of the Usual Patterns

Any combination of events which is not typical or standard in your framework of references is cause for a red flag to go up for you. Each health professional and each professional person develops a standard of expected patterns of illness and therapeutic responses. We recognize syndromes, apply a therapy, and view the healing process from a background of personal and collective experience. If any portions "do not ring true," let that be a red flag for you. Information of this kind may actually come from an intuitive or "gut" level. If the health professional feels or senses that something is not right, he or she should heed that intuition and evaluate it. No harm can come from that, and much harm may be avoided.

Summary of Red Flags' Importance

Each healing system and each person working within any healing system has a particular bias. My bias is that Western medicine is our major health care system in this country and that whenever in doubt, we must draw on its resources. The above guidelines are to help orient the alternative health care practitioner to the medical community; they are not meant to imply that allopathic medical care is necessarily superior. A list of red flags could easily be designed for the medical community as to when to draw on the resources of the alternative health care professions. The underlying issue is that the practitioner be of maximal service and do no harm.

Communication in the Therapeutic Setting

Empowerment

The words we use as practitioners can have at least as powerful an effect on our clients as a medication or therapeutic procedure. Clear, meaningful, positive communication is part of optimal health care. Once a person is licensed as a physician or recognized as a health professional or healer, historically and culturally he or she is "empowered." The community, the legal world, the suffering person, and his or her family all augment this authority. It is such a potent force that the health professional must recognize and consciously accept that this power has been bestowed even though it was not actually sought. By its nature, this empowerment process involves both our conscious and unconscious levels. Because this issue of empowerment is too often subordinate to the skills and degrees earned, and not something actively pursued, its existence and ramifications are often not fully or consciously recognized. The health professional is frequently unaware or in the course of a busy professional life has forgotten the magnitude of this empowerment. As a result, this authority may become an actual health hazard. Let us explore why this is so.

Beneath the level of exercising learned skills and professional conduct lies the more subtle issue of interaction between therapist and client, a factor which directly and profoundly affects the course of health and illness. Words, suggestions, attitudes, and gestures coming from an empowered source, all imprint on formative levels of the body, mind, and spirit of the person seeking help. The internal world of the client is strongly affected by the professional's words and their implications. For example, if a person has a chronic illness which is not life threatening, and perhaps relatively unimportant, such as some cases of allergy, having a doctor say that "nothing can be done for you," or "you must live with this the rest of your life" can literally undermine a person's foundation. Depression, anxiety, and a worsening of the illness can result from such remarks. Even more important, as a person envisions something as hopeless or beyond any hope of a cure, that "truth" will tend to manifest. We may be limited and chained by one vision just as we may be expanded and freed by another. As health professionals we must be aware of the impact of our comments, gestures, attitudes, and casual remarks on the client's psyche. How much better if the doctor had said, "There is nothing more that I can do for you."

A commonly repeated situation which I have encountered in my practice has motivated me to write these comments: a person with a recent onset of back pain, of perhaps one to two weeks duration, has X-rays taken which indicate a chronic degenerative change such as osteoarthritis or narrowing of disc spaces. Many practitioners credit the body pain to the X-ray findings, explaining and showing these findings to the patient as the cause of the problem. The fallacy is that the pain has been going on for one to two weeks, whereas the changes noted in the X-rays have been present for a number of years. The person may walk into the doctor's office with a simple back strain from lifting incorrectly, and walk out with a "degenerative disc disease" or "osteoarthritis of the spine." The seed is planted. The person has been given an illness which may occupy his or her consciousness for life, yet *which was not the cause* of the pain in the first place. In my experience, a strong correlation does not always exist between X-ray findings and the degree of pain or dysfuntion of part of the body. X-rays often do not stand on their own but should be viewed in the light of the person's history and complaint.

Empowerment of the health professional is enhanced by the emotional instability inherent in the role of being a patient. Feeling insecure about health, the patient has sought out another person for help. With self-confidence shaken, all incoming information is more heavily weighted. Moreover, depending on the fears, doubts, and other emotional issues that the patient is struggling with, there is great likelihood the patient will distort or not hear the information. As health professionals, our communication with the patient is part of the healing relationship. Double care must be taken to give clear information and imagery. Here, as elsewhere in our treatment, we must let the tenet "do no harm" guide us.

Language of Health

The practitioner can help patients develop healing attitudes toward their illness or problems by taking care to create ideas, mental images, and perceptions that reflect positively rather than make them the victims of the illness. The study of biofeedback has shown that the body responds to language and imagery. Most of us cannot tap directly into the autonomic nervous system on a conscious level. We cannot "tell" our blood pressure to fall or our hands to be warm, but these things can be accomplished, with training, if proper images are created in the mind. Internal imagery affects the unconscious mind and the autonomic nervous system because these systems cannot distinguish between real or imagined events. Dr. Carl Simonton has demonstrated the power of imagery in treating cancer, as has Dr. Gerald Jamposky at his Center for Attitudinal Healing.

Just as imagery can foster healing, it can also cause problems and illness. The unconscious mind has no sense of innuendo, no sense of humor, and no sense of time. Because the unconscious is so literal, people often unknowingly give themselves auto-suggestions or create mental imagery which limits their health or their abilities. This is important to understand when working with a person and ascertaining behavioral patterns and mental attitudes that may unknowingly affect the person in a negative way.

Four commonly used *words* bear mentioning here: The first word is "try." One implication of the word "try" is "not to succeed." A person who wants to quit smoking who says "I will *try* to quit" is giving a message to the unconscious nervous system that an effort or attempt will be made, but that it will not be successful. This is a double message and makes the task more difficult.

The second mixed message is "cannot." Confusion here is that people often use the word "cannot" when they really mean "will not." None of us can physically jump from the earth to the moon, so the statement "I cannot jump to the moon" is a true and honest statement. Statements such as "I cannot lose weight," on the other hand, are usually not literal, although that is the message that the unconscious hears. Far better to say "I will not lose weight," or "I have not been able to lose weight." It is extremely difficult to do something that you have told your unconscious mind that you cannot do; it is a disempowering statement.

A third word to be aware of is "should." The word implies an authority outside yourself, an edict somewhere that your behavior "ought not" to be what it is or "should be" something other than it is. If we habitually live in the world of "shoulds," we diminish our self-will, our self-control, and our mastery of the moment. Even if the action which the "should" suggests is totally correct, it is still preferable to make the statement or do the action without the use of the word itself. For instance, you "should" look both ways before crossing the street. This is good advice and true information. However, just to state "look both ways before crossing," gives the power to the individual and not to an outside authority.

The fourth word is not so much a mixed message to the unconscious as it is a mixed message on the conscious level. The word is "but." This is a perfectly "good" and important word which negates or diminishes everything that precedes it in a sentence. It is only when "but" is used in error, when the person really meant to use the word "and," that it becomes confusing. The word "and" continues a thought, moves it forward, while "but" shifts the direction of the idea or thought.

Separation of Cause and Effect

Unless it is absolutely necessary, do not interlock symptoms or complaints with the aging process. Any symptom which is linked to aging will be with the person for as long as he gets older, which of course, is for the rest of his life. Listen to a person as he recounts his history or symptomatology. If the patient makes innocent statements such as "it is tough to get old" or "I am not as young as I used to be" or "I feel like an old man (or woman)," it usually means that in his own mind, at least part of the problem is associated with age. Make an effort to defuse such remarks whenever possible. If you are able to disassociate the two and let the illness or symptom stand apart, not related to getting older, a greater potential for improved health exists.

For an empowered person to casually drop a remark like "it's tough to get old" to a patient in relation to a simple ache or pain is immoral. I have seen a number of people who begin to improve immediately once they understand that their "bursitis" or back pain is a matter of stress, weather, or injury, and not a matter of aging. Problems which have plagued them for a long time, and which have been credited to aging by another well-meaning person, have resolved. Perhaps more significant, their sense of well-being, vitality, and self-confidence returns as they are freed from the concept of "getting old."

Just as the physician can support and encourage health by dissociating symptoms from age, it is also supportive of health to separate symptoms from named disease processes. Saying "my shoulder hurts" is a statement of fact; it describes the here-and-now and has no further implication. Saying "my arthritis hurts" reinforces the illness, planting the idea more firmly in one's mind that the arthritis is a part of the patient almost the way an arm is one's arm or a leg is one's leg. Even when the named disease *is* the cause of the discomfort, it is healthier to just describe the symptom, to say only that one's arm hurts.

Affirmations

Pictures, goals, and ideas which are implanted in our minds tend to become self-fulfilling prophecies. The body literally takes such statements or mental pictures as truths and functions to manifest them as realities. Used creatively, affirmations such as "Every day and every way I am getting better and better," or "I see myself as being totally healthy and productive," or "Today is today and I'm glad it's today," establish unconscious programs which lead a person to a fuller, more active and creative life.

I have many patients who verbally affirm good health by repeating affirmations aloud each morning as part of their preparation for the day. The effectiveness of affirmations is greatly enhanced when they are spoken out loud, and repeated a number of times. Actually listening and hearing the message engages another part of our minds and imprints more deeply. To truly "hear" the message may require five, ten, or more repetitions.

Creating a Healing Perspective

The last general area for discussion is the importance of maintaining a clear, undistorted perspective of the health care world. Too many health care practitioners become negatively conditioned toward healing systems other than their own. Part of this prejudicial conditioning comes from overt teachings during the educational process. Part of this is that each of us attracts new patients from that group of people who are dissatisfied with their current care, or who have run a gamut of therapies and are still not well. This select sampling of dissatisfied people is not representative of the general population. If all day long a health care practitioner sees people who, for instance, state that a specific health system has not helped them or has actually caused them problems, the practitioner can easily feel that that system is inadequate or even destructive. Remembering that the patient sampling is not representative of all people helps to keep a practitioner from forming unjustified opinions based on a biased sample.

Other professionals see our failures just as we see theirs. Judging one another from dissatisfied clients tends to alienate and splinter the healing professions, making us critical of one another, and doing little to build respect and harmony in the healing world. If we look at a broader sampling of people or perhaps spend time observing other types of practices, seeing their approach and their results, and hearing the comments of their satisfied patients, we will have a truer viewpoint of other professions.

The medical profession and the alternative healing world have different perspectives of health and illness. In the former, illness is generally considered as an event; once the illness is over, the problem is gone. They do not envision the "healing process" itself. In natural healing, illness is viewed as part of a broader process in the person's life. The illness is seen as having a long preamble and an epilogue, and its own evolution (Herring's Law of Cure) as it resolves. The interpretations of symptoms can therefore be radically different for the two viewpoints. To a person in the natural healing schools, a rash which develops in an asthmatic patient who is improving may represent a healing crisis, proving the person is getting well and should not be treated. The same rash to a medical person may represent a symptom of illness or a complication of the treatment, and be treated as a pathology.

By the same token there is the view in Western medicine that certain conditions are lifelong and require ongoing medication. A person diagnosed as having essential hypertension is placed on medication with the assumption that the condition is permanent. Natural healing systems may view it as a reflection of an underlying stress or energy imbalance in the person's immediate life process and envision the person as having a normal blood pressure at a later date.

The Healing Vision

Dr. Yeshi Donden, a renowned Tibetan physician, told the traditional acupuncture conference (Washington, D.C., 1984) that a person should become enlightened before she or he becomes a health care practitioner. He defined enlightenment as the embodiment of four characteristics: love, compassion, joy, and impartiality. He went on to point out the great difference in attitudes between the sick person and the healer: "In the imagination and perception of the healer, the universe is a different universe (from the one) of hopelessness and impossibility of the patient; it is the universe of potentiality, a universe of possibility."

Professor Jack Worsley teaches acupuncturists to see deeply enough into a person to see that person's health, essence, and full health potential; "to see the dawning light" is an ingredient in healing.

If in the process of therapy with a client we begin with a vision of potentiality and possibility, and then in the course of treatment lose that vision, our healing effectiveness for that person will be vastly reduced. If we are unable to regain the positive vision, to reenter "the universe of potentiality and possibility," it is time to refer the patient to another practitioner. To fulfill the essence of the Hippocratic oath, and to justify our empowerment as health practitioners, we are charged to hold the vision of another person's health and welfare until that person can see the vision as well.

6
Bridges of Speculation

The growing edge of knowledge lies somewhere between fact and fiction.

The ideas in this chapter on energy-physiology are neither fact nor fiction. Rather, they are speculations on the mechanisms which promote homeostasis or balance in the relationships between energy and the physical body.

In his book *Science of Homeopathy*, George Vithoulkas states:

> The vital force of the human organism, in terms of electrodynamic vibration . . . involves a tremendous degree of complexity. The resultant vibration of such a complex organism is . . . highly complicated, changing from moment to moment, not only in frequency, but also in regularity of frequency and amplitude as well. The vital force level of the human organism is considered the "dynamic plane" affecting all levels of the being at once . . . . There are laws and principles governing both morbidic and therapeutic influences on this system.

Energy and Movement

Fundamental to these laws and principles is the underlying realization that *movement* is an inherent characteristic of energy. Movement comes in many forms — the vibration of individual subatomic particles; coordinated movement of organ system currents; and shifts in the relationships of one system to another.

Movement in the subtle body is stimulated and nurtured in a number of ways. It is stimulated on the mechanical level by physical movement; respiratory motion; the heart beat; bowel peristaltic motions; and the movement of blood, lymph, and other body fluids. It is also stimulated by the generation of friction force fields caused by the interfacing of moving substances (blood flowing through vessels, our body moving through air, and so on). On the electromagnetic level, the subtle body is influenced by the billions of electrical impulses in our nervous system. Energy is also directly supplied to the subtle body from sunlight, the metabolic and respiratory processes of the body, the vibratory input of our five senses, from the many chakras, the acupuncture point antennae, and the lightning rod function of the body.

Because the physical and subtle bodies are in constant resonance with each other, the vibrations of the *mind field* (our thoughts, mental processes, emotions, and visualization) affect the molecular structure of the body. This interaction helps account for the power and effectiveness of meditation and visualization, and supports fundamental principles of illness and healing. In *Toward a Future Medicine Based on Controlled Energy Fields,* William Tiller links Wolf's Law (of bone structure) to our mental fields:

> It is useful to recall Wolf's Law of bone structure: If one of our bones receives nonuniform stress for an extended period, the bone will grow trabeculae (a type of bone girder) in the exact location needed to support this stress distribution. The physical strain field probably interacts with the electrostatic field of the system producing changes, and these changes cause ions and molecules to be carried to specific locations.... Carrying this idea further, we can think of mental field patterns as acting like a stress influencing the field term of the magnetochemical potential of the molecules.

Movement and vibration in the subtle body are further influenced by factors existing outside the body. Such factors include temperature and humidity, biological clocks (time of day, season of the year), and celestial events. There are many relationships between the celestial bodies and planet earth, such as the gravitational pull of the moon affecting all water levels. New relationships, such as the effect of "sun spots" on behavior or the lack of sunlight causing depression, continually emerge.

An interesting experiment was done relating to the impressionability of the sunlight on water. [1] The experiment consisted of agitating containers of water exposed to the sun during different periods of a solar eclipse. The results of the experiment hold significant, even profound, implications for me regarding the imprinting of vibration on our subtle bodies. In the experiment, a number of identical jars of water were set in the sunlight prior to a solar eclipse. During the eclipse, at each fifteen minute interval, a different jar of water was agitated. At the conclusion of the solar eclipse, seeds were placed in each container and their growth rate charted. A graph of the growth rate showed decreased sprouting of the seeds in water that was agitated toward the center of the eclipse. The sprouting increased as the eclipse concluded. The significant variables were the agitation of the water and the period of the eclipse. Theodore Schwenk uses the experiment to demonstrate the impressionability of water to sunlight. I have often speculated in my medical practice whether agitated vibrations in a person's subtle body may also make them more impressionable. As I have mentioned, two seemingly similar injuries often respond totally differently to therapy. One variable seems to be the amount of stress (i.e., vibrational agitation) the person was under at the time of the accident.

Homeostatic Relationships

Even though the number of influences on our vibration is legion, it is helpful to speculate on several specific issues. According to Tradi-

1 Theodore Schwenk, *Sensitive Chaos: The Creation of Flowing Forms in Water and Air* (New York: Schocken Books, 1976), 65.

tional Chinese Medicine, we receive a quantum of ch'i energy at the time of our conception, which is nurtured during our lifetime from the ch'i in the food we eat and in the air we breathe.

The relationships of these two nurturing sources of ch'i with each other and with the ancestral ch'i are very complex, as are the metabolic processes involving oxygen and food stuffs in human physiology. My medical and energetic understanding has led me to assume that there is a simplistic homeostatic relationship between the need for vibration from food and the need for vibration from air, just as there is a direct relationship between food we metabolize and the air (oxygen) we consume. There is also a simplistic relationship between the vibration of food and the calories of food, and the vibration of air and the oxygen in air. The body has four different requirements, all of which are homeostatic relationships, any one of which can stimulate body response.

Homeostatic Relationships

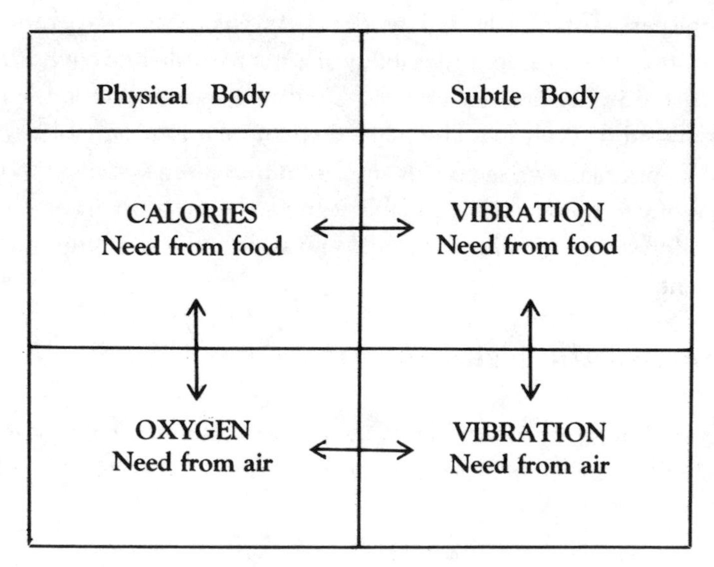

Whichever of these four needs is most urgent will provide the primary stimulation to the gastrointestinal and respiratory systems of the body. In the physical body, blood gas levels, mostly oxygen and carbon dioxide, regulate respiration; factors including stomach contractions, blood sugar levels, and thirst dictate the need to eat and drink.

In the energy body, the moment to moment vibratory needs stimulate the respiratory mechanism. The body's need for vibration can be most quickly met through the vibration of the air molecules. The underlying sustaining vibrations are met through the vibrations of the molecules in food and liquids. These affect the body more slowly because they must be processed through the gastrointestinal and metabolic systems. Once in the body their effect is more prolonged and sustained. We utilize both sources in a balanced manner to maintain body vibration, although as we shall see later, on different occasions we may rely more heavily on one system than the other.

The Body's Mechanisms for Regulating Energy

To more fully appreciate the body's homeostatic mechanisms and its ability to regulate vibration it is helpful to explore our physical anatomy. In relation to the respiratory system the naso-pharynx is of particular importance. This is the first portion of the respiratory system through which air must pass on its way into the body. Inside each of the

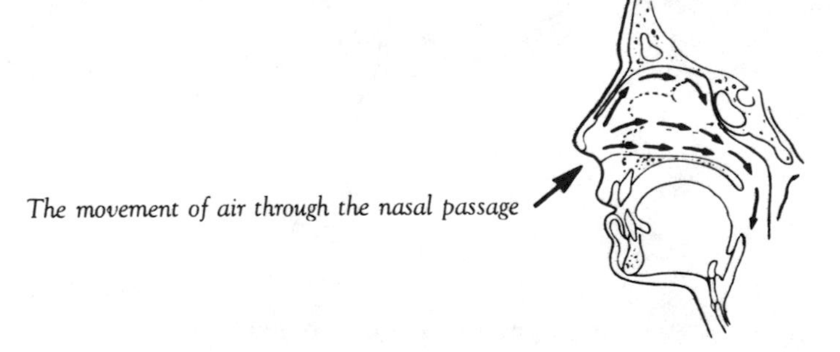

The movement of air through the nasal passage

nostrils are three passageways (upper, middle, and lower), created by mucosal folds known as turbinates. Which of these channels the air flows through will determine the exact direction of the movement of air from the front of the face to the back wall of the pharynx. Air which gets into the superior passage flows upward and stimulates the sense of smell and is then redirected, or turns a corner, to flow back down into the windpipe and lungs. At the top of this superior chamber is the cribriform plate, which supports the organ of smell and separates the nasal cavity from the frontal portion of the brain. Within the plate itself are a number of small air cells. On the upper side of the cribriform plate

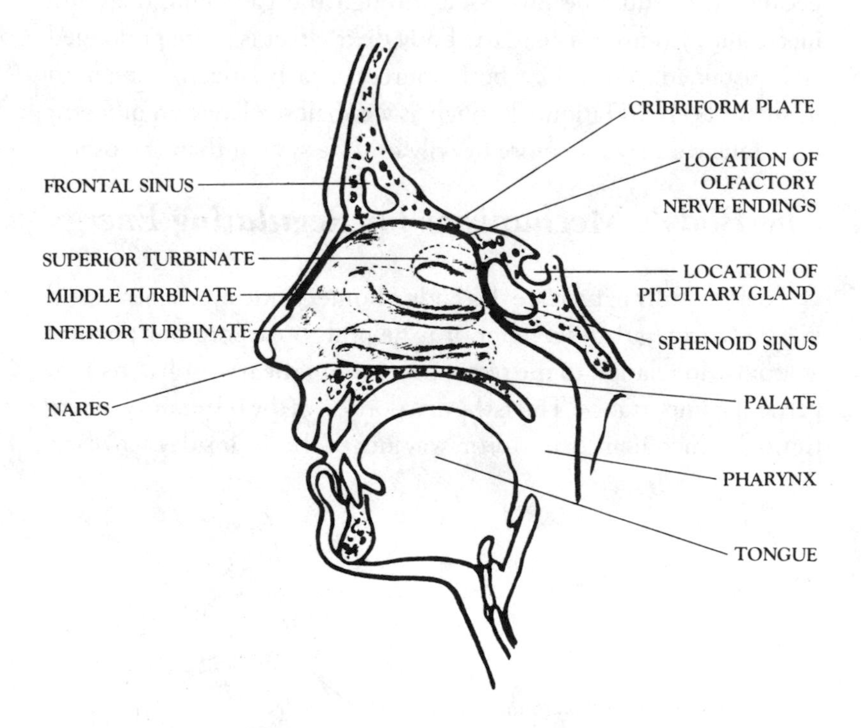

Side view of nasal cavity and related structures

is a bony ridge, to which one of the supporting structures of the brain, the falx cerebri, attaches. The cribriform plate, as well as the olfactory nerve, is stimulated by air moving through the superior nasal passage as it is reflected downward into the lungs.

Within the naso-pharynx are four major sinus cavities: the frontal, ethmoid, sphenoid, and maxillary. They all have communicating openings into the main nasal passages and are lined with a mucous membrane contiguous with the walls of the nose. There is a free flow of air and fluid between the sinus and nasal passages. As air enters the nose, a portion of it enters, fills, and leaves each sinus cavity.

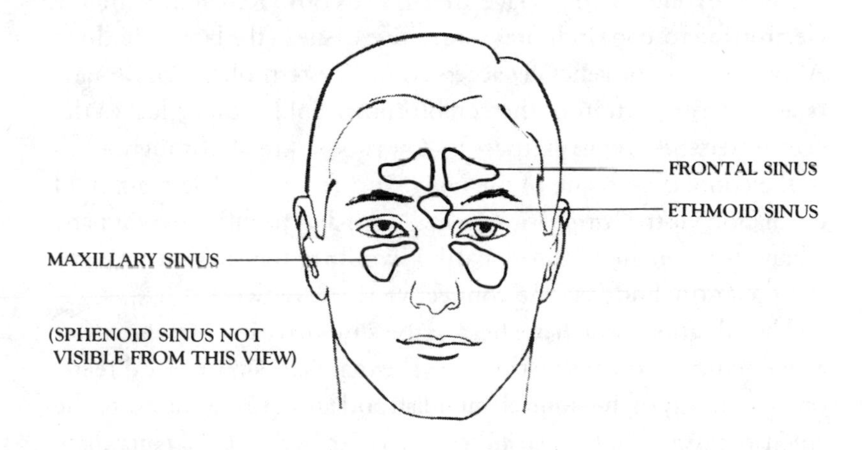

The major sinus cavities

The bony walls of the sinuses and air cells are very thin, and the entire sinus mechanism acts as a resonator and amplifier for the vibration and molecular movement of the air contained in the cavities. We have all experienced dullness and lifelessness in our face associated with colds or sinus infections when the sinuses are congested and we lose the feeling of the bone vibration.

The sinus cavities are filled with air, and the bony resonance and amplification of that air's vibration affects contiguous structures. The frontal sinus occupies the area above and between the eyebrows where the sixth chakra or "third eye" resides. The ethmoid air cells and those in the cribriform plate are adjacent to the brain. The sphenoid sinus and air pockets are in relation to the pituitary gland, which rests in a cavity within the sphenoid bone and is surrounded by the sphenoid air pockets.

A number of the bony surfaces of the sinuses are exposed to the cerebrospinal fluid surrounding the brain, so that the vibration in the sinuses directly affects this fluid. The cerebrospinal fluid cushions the spinal cord as well as the brain, and extends for a distance along each of the nerve roots as they leave the spinal cord. Research with the electron microscope indicates connective tissue of the body is hollow. Although it is not generally accepted in Western physiology, many believe that a portion of the cerebrospinal fluid actually leaves the central nervous system via these hollow tubes, spreads throughout all of the connective tissue of the body, and returns to the main fluid circulation via the lymphatic system. According to this viewpoint any vibration within the cerebrospinal fluid would be transmitted throughout the entire body via the connective tissue network.

The vibrations which are held in the sinus cavities may also affect acupuncture meridians on the face. The maxillary sinuses are directly on the pathway of the stomach meridian and are in juxtaposition to the colon meridian. The frontal sinuses are crossed by the bladder meridian, and almost all of the deep connecting pathways of the face are in relation to one or more of the sinus cavities. Through these meridian pathways vibrations may be brought directly into the energy body.

Breathing Rhythm

It is commonplace for one nostril to be more open than the other. According to Western medical physiology both nostrils should function equally and any deviation from this is away from normal. Some believe, however, that the inequality of nasal potency is not only normal, but that in a well-balanced, perfectly functioning body, there is a natural rhythm of three to four hours in which we alternate our predominant breathing from one nostril to the other. Each nostril can have a greater or smaller capacity to conduct air depending on the congestion of the turbinates. According to my understanding of energy physiology, the narrowing of the passages may serve an important homeostatic function.

Yoga Breathing Techniques

One well-known yoga breathing technique is the alternative breath. Sitting quietly, close the right nostril and inhale through the left. Close the left nostril and exhale through the right, then inhale through the right and exhale through the left. Continue this cycle for ten rounds. In *The Complete Book of Yoga,* Swami Vishnudevanda states that this breath pattern calms a person, balances and cleanses the deep energy pathways along either side of the spine (the Ida and Pingala), and harmonizes the functions of the left and right sides of the brain. (The frontal lobes of the brain are in juxtaposition to the upper side of the cribriform plates.)

Venturi Tubes

The narrowing of air passages in the nose creates a *venturi tube.* According to physics, a venturi tube exists when we reduce the size of an opening or openings through which a liquid or gas flows without reducing the volume of the substance passing through in the same period of time. If we move the same amount of liquid or gas through a small orifice in the same amount of time, it must move at a faster speed. When we are watering the garden with a hose and put our thumb over the nozzle, we are reducing the size of the opening without reducing the amount of water passing through. This causes the water to move through the opening at a higher velocity, evidenced by the fact that the water projects farther.

The smaller we make the opening, the farther we can squirt the

Venturi tube: the same amount of liquid or gas passing through smaller openings in the same period of time

water. This water has an increased velocity and a faster molecular vibration. It is these effects of the venturi tube which are of special interest to us here.

Speculation on the Breath And Molecular Vibration

Clinically, one of the earliest signs of vibratory deficiency is mild, usually unnoticed nasal congestion. The turbinates become slightly engorged with blood, narrowing one or both of the nasal passages, and create a venturi tube. The respirator muscles need to work harder to bring in the air through the narrowed nasal passage, just as the thumb had to work harder over the hose nozzle to project the water. According to the principle of conservation of energy, the additional velocity and vibration of the air and water comes from the additional work of the respiratory muscles and the thumb. This air moves at a higher velocity and greater molecular motion: it is "energized." Once in our systems it increases the overall vibration of the body. The depletion of the energy body is thus offset, the turbinates decongest, and the nasal passages open. This subtle venturi tube mechanism acts as a vibratory "thermostat." The size of the nasal passage adjusts in accordance with our "vibratory needs" and in relationship to the three or four hour nasal breath rhythm. Changing of the nasal membranes is one of the body's first responses to maintain homeostasis of molecular vibration within the energy body.

If the very mild turbinate congestion is inadequate to fill the vibratory need, further congestion will develop. There is a limit to this, however, because if the turbinates congest too much they will close off the nasal passage. Thus if the "stuffy nose" phenomenon is inadequate to replenish the vibrations of our body, or if the physical body needs more oxygen, a yawn reflex may develop. The yawn creates a larger venturi tube than that in the nose. A much greater volume of air, with increased velocity, comes into our bodies through the narrowed orifice of the pharynx, increasing both the oxygen and the molecular vibration. Even though we associate a yawn with fatigue, the first response to the yawn is to feel more energized rather than less, which in many cases wakes us up.

If we care to give ourselves an instant "vibratory pickup," we can make a short sniffing action. Here we are creating the venturi tube effect, not by closing a nostril but by increasing the amount of air going through the same-sized orifice. The sniff needs to be strong enough to be audible. Immediately following one, two, or three sniffs, one often feels a tingling or chill moving through the body, as the increased vibration passes into the subtle body. A pause may follow the sniff before the next inhalation because the need for vibration has been momentarily supplied by the increased velocity of the air, reducing the stimulus for activating the next breath.

A sidelight of nasal physiology concerns the erectile tissue of the nose. When a person becomes sexually aroused, not only the genital areas, but also the turbinates of the nose become blood-engorged. The nasal engorgement creates a venturi tube, increasing the vibration in the energy body at a time when it is needed to match the excitement of the individual. This is another mechanism to maintain homeostasis.

Speculation on Food and Molecular Vibration

The vibration that food provides has different characteristics than that provided by the breath. The vibration contained in food is more varied and complex than the vibration received from the air and requires a longer period to become available to the subtle body since the food must be digested, absorbed, and metabolized. The release of food's vibration is gradual and sustained over a longer period of time, and provides a stable complex base for the subtle body. Our more immediate and spontaneous needs for vibration are monitored and met through the breathing process; our background sustaining vibration is provided by food.

Despite the basic difference of air and food in terms of vibratory function and complexity, there is a homeostatic relationship between them in which one acts as a "back-up system" for the other. For short periods, if necessary, the spontaneous vibratory need can be supplied by food just as for short periods this sustaining vibration can be maintained by air. If, however, we depend on the reserve capacity of either system for too long, it affects our stability and alertness and the physiology of the body.

The range of vibrations varies from food to food as well as with food preparation. As a general statement, the more highly processed and refined the food, the more the vibration is altered from the preprocessed original form. The caloric value may not be affected, and so it still meets the needs of the physical body, but the vibrational quality may be altered enough to affect the vibration of the subtle body.

Assume that a person primarily eats foods which fail to supply the full vibrational components to the subtle body. Gradually the sustaining energy of the body is diminished, which is reflexed as low reserve and ultimately an altered response to stress. Increasingly, the body calls on the backup system of the breath to provide the missing vibration. Because the breath is an ever-changing component, the nature of the air vibrations is inherently less stable than the vibrations from food, and as these temporarily fill the needs of the background vibration, a quality of instability, tentativeness, and imbalance is introduced into the already compromised background vibratory fields.

Caloric Highs and Vibratory Lows: New Perspectives on the Sugar Blues

The caloric needs of the body may be satisfied on a diet of processed sugars even though the sustaining vibratory requirements are not. The person gets a mixed message: on the one hand the body needs are being met; on the other hand they are not. The person's experience is that low grade fatigue and depression (resulting from incomplete vibration) is relieved by foods which are rapidly metabolized. The energy released from the processing of the high blood sugar overcomes the depressed feelings, but these foods do not have the vibration needed to sustain the subtle body. When the "caloric high" is over, depression and fatigue of low vibration once more occur. With the return of symptoms, more rapidly metabolized foods (simple sugars) are consumed, continuing the cycle of "caloric highs" and "vibratory lows." The wider these swings become, and the more the disparity between the metabolic and vibratory needs, the more the homeostatic mechanisms break down. Through misinterpretation of body messages, the person has adopted dietary habits which aggravate the problem rather than overcoming it. The longer this goes on, the more chaotic it can become, leading to serious physiological and psychological problems.

The Expanded State

In our normal daily activity food is the primary source of the sustaining vibration of the energy body. However, at times we extend ourselves to the point of "running on nervous energy," where breath dominates as the primary source of the sustaining vibration. Often these periods are associated with a strong emotional content. Emotions certainly affect the body's vibrations, but in and of themselves do not increase the body's overall energy. If the body needs more vibration to sustain an emotion, any one of a number of things may occur, including the increase of food intake (nervous eating) or accelerated breathing (hyperventilation).

When we are "running on nervous energy," or on an "emotional high," it is common to eat less. As the "high" continues the need for sleep diminishes, and the heightened emotional charge often produces feelings of high energy, euphoria, well-being, hope, and optimism; the expanded state.

During such a high, the effect of highly processed food may be more noticeable. This is especially true if the expanded state has continued over a period of time, depleting the physical body through lack of sleep and nutriment and causing the person to be "strung out," despite the sense of well being.

My first insight into the dynamics of this came when I was on an emotional high following a four-day conference. I felt euphoric and was enjoying my first substantial meal in all that time. Everything went well until the ice cream was served. After two spoonfuls, I began to collapse. Within just a minute or two I was unable to keep my eyes open to concentrate on the conversation, or even sit up in the chair. I felt so totally deenergized that I had to be driven home.

I usually eat all food with impunity, including ice cream. This was an unusual experience for me. I was intrigued by it and wanted to understand the mechanism behind it. In the months following I experimented with foods in an effort to understand what had happened. I found that in everyday situations where I have ample sleep and am eating well-balanced meals, highly-refined, processed, or simple sugar foods are no problem to me. When I am running on nervous energy and in a more delicate, heightened vibratory state, on the other hand, eating these foods rapidly lessens my elation and may cause depression. Months after my experience I heard Swami Muktananda tell how he had recommended the use of sugar to "bring down" a woman who had become too expanded during an intensive meditation.

Fasting

A state of well being can be created as well as diminished through food. Consider fasting. During a simple vegetable, fruit, or water fast, there is a typical progression which involves the body, mind and emotions. The actual fasting period, which may be anywhere from one to seven days or more, is preceded by several days of gradual reduction of the complexity of the usual diet. When the fast is complete, a period of days is required to once again introduce complex foods.

During the fast itself, especially if it is one's first or second time, a person may feel toxic for a period, often around the second day. Physically there may be backache, headache, strong urine and body odor, bowel change, and "furry" tongue. Emotionally one may experience depression, irritability, anger, sadness, or "clouded mentality." As this passes, feelings of physical and mental clarity, lightness, heightened sensitivity and awareness come, feelings of being "well" and "whole." Interestingly enough, hunger itself is rarely a problem while one is fasting. One criterion for actually ending a fast is when the hunger sensation begins to return; another is when the tongue is no longer "furry." Fasting has a cleansing effect on the physical body, as evidenced by the toxic period of the fast, and on the subtle body, as evidenced by the changes of emotion. On both levels, the end results are the expanded feelings of well being.

Complex Interactions of Energy Sources

The relationship of food to the body vibration involves a number of factors. A major factor is the type of food eaten and how it is processed and prepared. Other factors are the person's mental /

emotional state at the time of consumption, the condition of the physical and subtle body, the source of vibratory nurturing, and the state of consciousness.

Just as the breath can be the back-up vibratory support for food, food can be a back-up reserve for the breath. If a person's normal breathing mechanism is disrupted because of a chronic nasal or sinus infection, and the venturi mechanism is disturbed, the food reservoir support system may be activated. Food vibration along with air vibration comes into play for balancing our moment-to-moment emotional vibratory needs. The greater the dependence on food for this purpose, however, the more vulnerable a person becomes to the quality of the food ingested. A low vibrational food may cause mild depression when a person has a simple nasal problem, but not affect the person when in good health.

A more complicated situation is the effect of poor vibrational food on the person with chronic nasal-sinus condition. It works like this: a sinus infection occurs, rendering ineffective the various mechanisms which transfer air vibration from the nasal chamber into the body (venturi tube effect, sinus cavities, cribiform plate, cerebrospinal fluid, and so on). Because of the infection, the nasal pharynx is unable to supply a portion of the vibration to the body which is usually derived from the air. The body will turn to food vibration to compensate for this lack. In a healthy person, this lowers the burden on the naso-pharyngeal system and homeostasis results until the infection is cleared. However, if a person is habitually ingesting low vibrational foods, and may in fact already be relying to some extent on air vibration for support of his or her sustaining vibration, food-based vibration cannot compensate for the compromised naso-pharynx. Both systems become depleted. As this occurs, the nasal turbinates may further congest and the nasal stuffiness increases in an effort to activate the venturi mechanism. Now, instead of energizing the air, this complicates the sinus infection, further increasing the dependency on food; the compensatory activity has then become chronic and the person becomes food sensitive. This is actually the end result of the dissolution of the compensatory relationship between the nose and the alimentary canal.

In addition to any specific remedies, long-range self-help includes recharging both the respiratory and alimentary systems and strengthening their compensatory relationships. The respiratory system can be partially recharged by introducing mild aerobic exercises; the alimentary tract aided by improving the quality of food intake. Food which causes nasal stuffiness may represent "true" food allergy or be a food which is triggering the compensatory venturi tube nasal congestion.

Nasal Decongestants and Antihistamines

The effect of nasal decongestants is interesting. Part of nasal and sinus congestion may be due to pathology (trauma, infection, etc.), part may be due to the compensatory reaction of the body (the venturi tube mechanism), and part to the normal breath cycle of the nose. If the use of antihistamines or nasal drops makes an immediate and sustained improvement in a person's physical condition, probably the medication is offsetting the effects of the pathology itself. However, if a person improves for several hours following the use of the medication and then begins to notice fatigue or a recurrence of congestion relieved only by the use of more medication, the possibility exists of decompensation of a normal body process, or a tissue sensitivity if a topical medication is being used.

It is important to differentiate homeostatic nasal stuffiness from stuffiness caused by pathology. The implications for treatment are obviously totally different. Some antihistamines are known to cause side effects such as depression or drowsiness. If they are used to decongest homeostatic nasal congestion, the "side effects" may actually represent the "decompensation" of the body's attempt to create balance. In this respect they are not true side effects of the chemical itself. In evaluating any set of symptoms one needs to discern whether it represents pathology, an iatrogenic problem, a healing crisis (according to Herring's Law of Cure), a compensatory reaction of the body responding to another need, or simply an appropriate body response to a specific stimulus.

Body Compensations

When there is a chronic energy or vibratory deficiency, the body attempts to limit further loss. Any system of the body may reduce its function. The result might be shallow respiration, constipation, scanty and infrequent urination, sluggish gall bladder, dry skin, cold extremities, reduced sweating, diminished menstrual flow, and so on. On the behavioral level, we might see lethargy, fatigue, decreased libido, and general hypo-function.

If there is an excess of energy or vibration in the body, it may be dissipated by increased body functions. Hence, sweating, sneezing, coughing, diarrhea, runny nose, frequent urination, skin rashes, or heavy menses may occur. Behaviorally, the excess may be dispelled through laughter, crying, garrulousness, fidgeting, and hyper-functions of any sort.

On all levels, the body is continually engaged in activity leading toward balance and homeostasis. Checks and balances exist within each system, as well as between systems, and many of the homeostatic or compensatory responses result in a change of body function.

Disrupted Homeostasis

The American public is being conditioned to regard every change of body function as abnormal. We are taught to regard every stuffy nose or every instance of diarrhea or constipation as a condition which must be treated or medicated. This is not only incorrect information, but potentially harmful. Routinely medicating every symptom can actually interfere with the very mechanism that nature sets in motion to keep us well. Constantly treating these "symptoms" will upset the delicate homeostatic mechanisms within the body, leading to lowered resistance and poor health on all levels. Equally important, believing that these "symptoms" represent illness, creates the internal vision that every change of body function is a sickness. This suggests to the unconscious of a well person that he or she is sick, and these mental pictures and suggestions can set in motion cycles of self-fulfilling prophecies of illness.

The gastrointestinal system (stomach, small intestine, and colon) and respiratory system (nasal pharynx and lungs), although literally "inside" the body, represent bridges between the external world and our inner workings. Until a substance or gas has crossed an intestinal or respiratory membrane, it is not truly "within" the body. Symptoms that arise within these systems, especially in the early stages of an illness, may be attempts of the body to rid itself of potentially disease-causing materials prior to their absorption. Hence coughing, vomiting, and diarrhea may be serving the person's health.

Remember, that in addition to physical forces, excessive or deficient vibrations within the subtle body may affect the functions of any organ or system in an effort to release or contain energy. These compensatory functional changes should also not be viewed in and of themselves as illness, nor should the functional change be suppressed or altered. Look to the deeper cause of the imbalance and the "symptoms" will resolve. The philosophy of suppressing symptoms without considering and evaluating the underlying dynamic is contrary to good health and common sense.

Levels of Illness

In natural healing we speak of the "depth" of an illness or imbalance in terms of levels. The homeopathic hypothesis maintains that illnesses occur within energy levels or strata and that there are particular disease entities which are characteristic for each stratum. A very strong stimulus, in the form of either a disease or a therapeutic action can cause a quantum vibratory shift in the body from one energy stratum to another. At that new level, there again are a series of possibilities, but these will be different from the group of illnesses in that stratum from which the person has just moved. Obviously a person can move to a level closer to health or deeper into illness depending on the stimulus.

Within any given layer we can absorb minor shocks in the physical and energy body without alteration to our health. If our resistance is low or the stimulus excessive, however, the defenses of the physical or subtle body are overridden and symptoms develop within that layer. In more extreme situations, as noted above, a quantum shift of levels actually occurs where entirely different sets of problems prevail.

In my internship, a woman was brought into the hospital with a very severe asthmatic attack. Medication was administered to abort the attack. The following morning the asthma had totally abated but she had entered into a schizophrenic crisis. The shock of stopping the physical symptom had pushed the woman from one stratum of disease to another, although it may have saved her life as she was so critically ill the night before.

Herring's Law of Cure

Illness does not always occur or vanish suddenly; often an underlying process precedes the onset of symptoms and accompanies their resolution. This "process" may be considered speculative by very conservative health care practitioners, but in homeopathy and in many natural healing systems it is considered a major guideline for patient care. A prominent homeopath, Dr. Constantine Herring, summarized the healing process. This summary is referred to as Herring's Law of Cure and states that: a person heals from deep to superficial; from "more important" to "less important" organs and systems; old symptoms return in the reverse order of their occurrence; and we heal from the top of the body toward the feet.

Healing from deep to superficial has two ramifications. The first is the literal occurrence of symptoms deep in the body becoming more superficial. A high fever which breaks into profuse sweating is such an example. An example of the reverse, that is, the onset of an illness, might be a cold wind blowing on the neck which results in a deep muscle spasm in the neck.

The physical is considered the most superficial aspect, the mind / emotion deeper, and the spiritual aspect the deepest. In the healing process, when a person first gets a glimpse of getting well, has hope rekindled, or regains a spark for life, it means that the deepest level has been stirred and improved. From here the healing will move up to the emotional/mental realm and in its final stages be manifest in the physical body. If in the process of treatment a person feels physically better but is more despondent, this indicates that the process may be going in the wrong direction and the condition worsening. Both the diagnosis and treatment need reevaluation, despite the fact that the person feels better.

To understand the concept of healing passing from the "more important" to the "less important" organ or system, let us consider the following: Traditional Chinese Medicine considers the skin to be a third lung, since it performs a similar function in terms of breathing and excreting. If a person is being treated for asthma, and during the course of treatment the asthma improves but a skin rash develops, the person is experiencing the natural healing progression. The major organ has healed first (the lungs) and the lesser organ (skin) is manifesting some symptoms prior to complete recovery. The rash is good news.

It is an an accepted fact in Western medicine that a child who has atopic dermatitis may develop asthma later in life. The healing process is the reverse of that sequence. In this situation, where the patient requires education in healing principles. If the patient does develop a skin rash while recovering from asthma, the rash may represent a healing phenomenon, and if so, should be allowed to run its course. Treating the "rash of healing" with a suppressive drug such as cortisone is absolutely antithetical to the natural healing process: supressing this rash means blocking the road to health.

In the process of natural healing, old symptoms may return in the reverse order of their occurrence. When working with a person's energy system, if we see the return of problems or symptoms which the person had earlier in life, we consider this to be part of the healing process. These problems stem from imprints released from deep within the body and should not be suppressed.

I once saw a woman seeking help for migraine headaches. According to her history she had suffered bronchial asthma which had disappeared with adolescence. Before beginning acupuncture therapy,

I had reviewed with her the laws of healing. The night following the first treatment she had an asthma attack, the first one in over twenty years. Understanding that this was possible according to the laws of healing, she did not become frightened, nor did she treat the asthma, which passed in short order. This was the only sign of asthma she had throughout the entire course of acupuncture. Her migraines resolved.

Generally, symptoms returning from past history do not last long, perhaps several hours or a day or two. Occassionally, however, with a severe problem, they can last longer. One woman had asthma so severely that she had been on daily cortisone therapy for five years. In the course of her prolonged recovery she developed a generalized skin problem which lasted for two years. The asthma eventually improved and she was able to discontinue cortisone treatments.

In some cases, one principle of Herring's Law will be contrary to another. The woman being treated for migraine headaches who developed an asthma attack might be perceived as going from a superficial (headache) to a deeper problem in the body (asthma), or going from a less important symptom of headache to a more important symptom of breathing difficulties, which would be movement in the wrong direction. However, in this case, the principle of old symptoms returning superseded the other two principles. This was borne out later, as the asthma did not return and the headaches disappeared.

The skin has a dual position in the Law of Cure. It represents the superficial aspect of an organ system, the lungs, as well as the most superficial aspect of our body. Therefore, any skin rashes or skin problems that present themselves during the process of energy balancing or of natural healing deserve special attention. There is a corollary to Herring's Law: Cure proceeds by amelioration on internal planes coupled with the appearance of a discharge or eruption of skin or mucous membranes. [1]

It is naive and potentially dangerous, however, to say that every

1 George Vithoulkas, *The Science of Homeopathy* (Grove Press, Inc., 1980), 231. New York.

symptom appearing while a person is under therapy is a healing phenomenon, or that every skin rash is the Law of Cure. I was at a meditative retreat some years ago when a young man told me he was going through an internal cleansing process because of the depth of his meditation. I was curious and asked what the cleansing process was. He said that his deeper problems were moving to the surface and that he was developing a skin rash. When I examined the rash, it turned out that he had contracted scabies. I suggested that he go to the infirmary for some medication to limit the spread of the infestation.

The Healing Crisis

Professor Worsley, in the *Acupuncture Handbook*, states that nobody can be *cured* of a problem without having a healing crisis. During the course of energetic medicine, a patient may develop "the worst headache" or "the worst asthma attack" he or she ever had. In a healing crisis, ideally we do not treat the symptom; rather we let it run its course. But if the person must have assistance or treatment, the aim is to move forward *through* the problem and not to suppress or eradicate the symptom per se. The problem should be understood in its proper context in the healing crisis.

The healing crisis may first manifest on any level of the body, mind, or spirit. It may be experienced as a physical symptom, an emotional outburst, a sudden *Gestalt*, a dream or nightmare, or a revelatory sense of knowing. After one level is affected all the levels will be. In some cases there is an almost simultaneous occurrence in the body / mind / spirit.

I used acupuncture to treat a man with chronic diarrhea. He was improving gradually. After the eighth visit he had a bout of severe cramping and diarrhea and experienced profound sadness recalling an event from when he was five years old (the death of his dog), yet had the inner sense of knowing that he was well. These three incidents happened within a twelve hour period, after which the diarrhea was resolved.

The Autonomy of Illness

Once a disease process or imbalance in the body is established it becomes autonomous. Even though the problem may be contrary to the greater general health and balance of the individual, the problem has its own existence and is part of a larger process. The martial art of Aikido, a basically nonviolent martial art, emphasizes "lovingly helping your opponent to the ground." In dealing with a disease process or imbalance, we can recognize its independent existence and "lovingly" help it leave the body. This notion is more in harmony with natural healing than the "heroic" notion of "casting out" the disease. Even in those cases where we do need to violently dislodge a disease from the body, my experience has taught me that maintaining respect for the disease hastens the healing process.

Problems treated through natural healing systems may take longer to resolve as compared to the more dramatic, immediate response to drugs. Such a comparison however, may not always be either relevant or justified, because the variables are not the same. The strength of many drugs — and their emphasis — lies in suppressing or removing the symptom. In the natural healing orientation the emphasis is on supporting nature and the body's own recuperative powers, and monitoring the process of recovery. There is a balance and interface between the "health" and the "illness," and because of the autonomy of an established illness or imbalance, it also "wants" to exist. For a while the imbalance may come and go as the body mobilizes its forces around health. A sign of healing is that the problem recurs less often, less severely, and for a briefer duration. Even after a healing crisis, further time and aid are often required before nature resolves the problem. The issue of prevailing over disease and regaining health is a *process*, not an *event*, and as such requires time.

Attitude of Healing

As we observe a person going through the healing process over a period of weeks or months, it is beneficial to view the process from a detached viewpoint. Our responsibility is not to cure another person. The healing is done by nature and our responsibility is to support that process to the best of our skill and knowledge. By maintaining a noncritical, nonjudgmental attitude, we keep ourselves off the roller coaster of elation or depression depending on whether a person "gets better" or "gets worse." Ego-involvements with a client's healing process do not help the client and can actually decrease our effectiveness.

Pressure Gradient

The last general principle to mention in the physiology of the energy body is that whenever a person is in the state of abrupt change, he or she is more vulnerable to illness and more prone to accidents. This is known as "the pressure gradient." A common example is that of the person who has endured a long period of emotional stress, perhaps the prolonged illness of someone in the family or a divorce, and throughout the event itself has held up quite well. When the event is over and the pressure is off, the person becomes sick. A marked change or altered pressure causes a shift in the body. During these periods of shifting and reestablishing homeostasis, there is an inherent instability with greater vulnerability toward illness and accident. The body can stabilize around a constant stress. When the stress levels are changed there is a lack of stability.

Knowing that this pressure gradient exists allows one to prepare somewhat for the changes of stress levels. By taking extra care with rest, good nutrition, and avoiding new stresses, and by utilizing visualization, meditation, and energy balancing during the change from one level of pressure to another, one can emerge from this period without illness.

A New Understanding of Health and Illness

Physical anatomy and physiology are generally recognized, but the existence and significance of the energy or subtle body and its anatomy, physiology, and vibration are not widely appreciated. As we come to acknowledge its existence, the implications and conclusion we draw from events in our everyday lives and in the therapeutic setting are quite different from those formerly based on physical reality alone. Illness becomes a process and not an event. If a person can be shown how an accident or illness can serve as a teacher, the accident or illness can actually assume a role in the evolution and growth of the individual.

The principles of nature manifest on all levels, and as we seek deeper understanding of the hidden elements of a system, these principles expand our options. Once merged, the healing systems of East and West complement each other, bringing a new balance to our view of human health and healing. Understanding the natural balance of the subtle and physical bodies brings a new glimpse of the power to create health in ourselves and others.

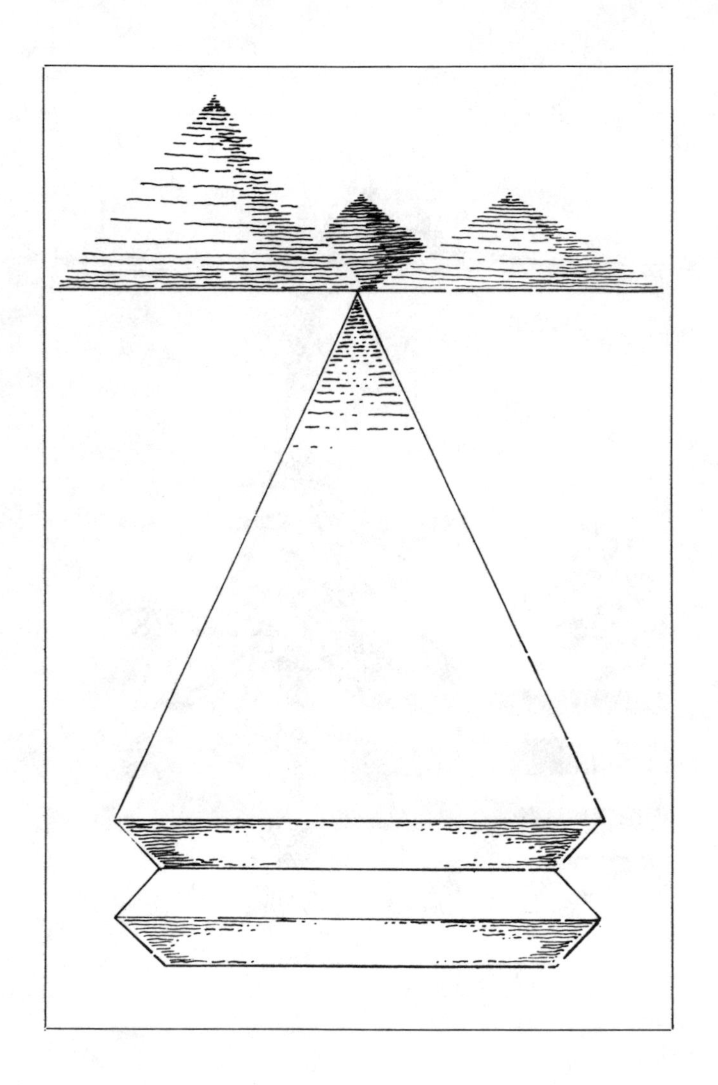

7

Bridges to the Future

What we nurture in ourselves will grow;
that is nature's eternal law. – Goethe

One of the natural laws in Chinese philosophy is that patterns and sequences recur throughout nature — on all levels of reality. The movement of the planets in the heavens is similar to the movements of electrons within atoms. As above, so below. The macrocosm is reflected in the microcosm.

We can observe and experience the movement inherent in many of these patterns — the fluctuation of temperature and humidity, the cycle of day and night, the changing of seasons of the year. We can appreciate much of the movement of nature as it interacts with the solid structure of the particle world — the wind bending blades of grass, the water currents molding rivers and streams, the growth of plants and trees enlivening the earth.

We cannot feel or touch or smell or taste many of the changing patterns of nature in the same way that we can the world of structure and objects, but that makes them no less significant in our lives. Many of the sequences are too slow (the formation of mountains), too fast (electron movement), too large (the currents within the ocean), or too small (cellular movement in the body) to observe directly — and yet we know they exist.

The Expanding Vision of the Human Body

For thousands of years the Eastern cultures have been developing and working with systems that directly address those subtle patterns in nature that affect our bodies and which are perceived primarily through subjective observation and experience. The subjective experience of the Eastern "scientists" is not wholly foreign to Western science. In modern physics researchers are finding that their attitudes and expectations affect the outcome of "objective" experiments, indicating a deep connection between the subjective and objective worlds. In medicine we are just beginning to understand the importance of our subtle nature, our relationship to it, and ways to evaluate and balance it.

In the first acupuncture workshop I attended in 1971, a man in his seventies had come to see Professor J.R. Worsley because of a condition in his right hand which prevented him from fully closing it into a fist. He had been having this problem for more than ten years, during which time he had been thoroughly examined by a number of physicians and at various medical centers. No treatment had been helpful.

I did not see his acupuncture treatment itself, but was present as he walked out of the consultation room, closing his hand fully for the first time in ten years. He was ecstatic. I was one of several acupuncture students who excitedly asked about the treatment: where had the needles been placed and did they hurt? I learned that only a single needle had been used and this had been placed in the soft tissue of the opposite leg. The needle was kept in place for about ten seconds, during which time the patient was unaware of any pain. As I listened to this treatment report my mind seemed to explode; none of my medical experience could account for what I was hearing. It was shortly thereafter that I committed myself to the study of energy and our subtle nature.

The struggle to resolve the apparent conflicts between my own scientific training and the teachings of the Eastern medical and energy models has been both challenging and creative. And I believe that my experience in this is not an uncommon one for many physicians and health practitioners raised and trained in the Western traditions. It is important to see that out of this struggle a new understanding of the human body is emerging along with a more complete model of health and healing. It is in the service of this expanding vision that I have written *Inner Bridges*.

A Review of the Working Energy Model

The patterns and sequences of movement which occur in the human body are exceedingly complex. To make the knowledge of these patterns useful, I have simplified, perhaps even oversimplified, the total picture by dividing it into functional increments. These increments have been reassembled to produce a grid or structure on which to organize my knowledge and experience and expand with them.

The working energy model of the human body is composed of three functional units: first, the nonorganized background field of energy; second, the vertical movement of current conducted through the body which orients us to our environment; and, third, the internal flows of the body which are produced because of the body's unique and individualized presence and which organize us into discrete functioning units. This last pattern — energy flows within the body— is further divided into three levels: the deep current through the bone and skeletal system; the middle currents through the soft tissues of the body; and the superficial level of vibration beneath the skin surface. All of these flows and vibrations intermingle and interrelate, but there is sufficient autonomy that we can delineate specific functions and recognize discrete characteristics of each of the three levels.

Amplification of the Model

In this book I have chosen to expand and amplify this basic model through the discussion of Yoga and acupuncture and to indicate how knowledge of these systems feeds back into the basic energy pattern.

Many of the other systems of natural healing — homeopathy, the Hawaiian Kahuna beliefs, and the American Indian mythology, to name just a few — could also be related to this model and would further expand its potential usefulness.

Implementation of the Model

The metaphor I use of "bridging" seems highly appropriate when considering the body in terms of the structural and energetic components. Bridges within each of us make connections between our own structure and our own vibratory nature. Bridges connect us to the whole of nature, and there are bridges across which one person can contact another person's structure and vibration.

I have indicated that vibratory fields and current can be contacted in a number of ways: by the hands, by needles, by a variety of physical modalities (heat, cold, ultrasound), through body posture (Hatha Yoga), through visualization, meditation, diet, and so on. My particular interest has been the use of the hands and establishing direct contact with the physical structure and the vibratory components.

By the use of movement (traction, pressure, bending, twisting) and by the use of nonmovement (the fulcrum) we can feel another person's body stretch and resist as it relates to our forces. We can assess its clarity, density, and pliability. A certain amount of movement or suppleness of the energy body is necessary for optimum health. Too little results in rigidity, lack of response, and proneness to those injuries inherent in any brittle or rigid structure. Too much movement results in instability, lack of personal power, suggestibility, and a whole list of injuries that are common to hypermobile structures.

The characteristics of a person's energy can be further assessed through the speed with which it responds to our needles, pressures, and fulcrums — how quickly the person develops REMs or breath patterns, or shows other signs of energy movement in reference to the energetic stimulus. The locations of energetic excesses or deficiencies provide additional insights into a person's inner world. We can interpolate through our knowledge of energetic grids: security relates to the pelvic bowl, sexuality to the sacrum, power to the lumbar area, anger and frustration to the hips and jaw, compassion to the heart, sadness to the chest, creativity to the throat, and intuition to the brow. These are broad generalizations, but are useful in taking us across to the physical-emotional (energetic) nature of the person.

Just as there are many ways to evaluate the energy body of a person, there are many ways to balance and clear it. Examples include body work, acupuncture, herbology, movement therapy, direct energy balancing, and visualization. Inherent in many of these approaches are the involuntary responses of the client to energy movement through which we can objectively monitor their process. In hands-on body balancing systems, we have the additional feedback of what we actually feel through our hands.

All of these guidelines give tangibility to energy work and ground us in skills which might otherwise be elusive and vague, highly vulnerable to the distortions of the imagination. The guidelines for working with energy become even more solid and useable if there is some theoretical understanding of the involuntary responses of the client (such as apneas, hyperpneas, REMS) and the relationship of vibration and movement to the physical body.

Complementary Views of Disease

As one accepts energy into a view of health and disease, it becomes clear that all illness has an energetic manifestation and that it is possible to account for disease in terms of "energy imbalance." However, it is specious to assume that *all* problems are originally energetic in nature just as it is specious to assume that all problems are basically physical in nature. For example, there is no question that there is an energetic component to a fractured ankle, but the primary structural pathology is that of the bone and not the disruption of the energy pathways. The primary care is medical, the secondary care is energetic. On the other hand, a functional problem, such as asthma or colitis, may have a medical component, but the primary pathology is, more often than not, the response to life stress. In this case the fundamental care may be energetic or psychological and the symptomatic care allopathic.

The alternative health care systems and the allopathic medical model often address different needs. Rather than being mutually exclusive, they can be used in a complementary fashion. They represent different chapters in the same book of health and wholeness.

The Unfolding Life Process

I recently heard a presentation of Holistic Depth Psychology by Dr. Ira Progoff.[1] According to Progoff, the unconscious portion of our minds not only represents the "repressed" contents of the personality as described by Sigmund Freud, and the "collective unconscious," as described by Carl Jung, but it also contains a portion of the person's potential which has yet to blossom.

Progoff likens this potential portion of the unconscious to the seed of a plant whose growth is determined not by the past experiences of the personality, but by the teleological goals inherent within the species. This portion of the mind is unconscious not because it is suppressed, but because the time has not yet come for its unfolding in the person's life. This unfolding has its own timetable. It is the buried future which will emerge as the life progresses.

As I listened to Progoff, it seemed apparent to me that as this seed potential manifests, it will be expressed *through* the existing framework of the person's current world view and the vibration and structure that is present in the body/mind/spirit at that time. The unfolding of the potential within the unconscious follows a natural order and has parallels to the yogic understanding of the activation of the main chakras of the body. In both cases, the "unfolding" is manifest through the environment of the person's body/mind/spirit as it exists at that particular moment.

In ancient India, the yogi aspirant spent many years in the process of internal purification in preparation for the activation of the chakras

1 Dr. Ira Progroff, *The Waking Dream and the Living Myth in the Creative Work of Ingmar Bergman*, (New York City: Federation for the Arts, Religions and Culture in New York City, a Dialogue House Recording).

through the awakening of the kundalini. The internal clarity that resulted from this preparation helped the person to accommodate the amplified energy released within the body, minimizing kriyas and any illness, confusion, or psychosis that might result.

In our culture today, there is generally less preparation for the activation of the chakras or the opening of the deep unconscious processes as described by Progoff. For some people these life events are easy, natural, and almost effortless; for others they may be traumatic, frightening, alienating, or disruptive. One of the variables affecting how people react to their unfolding is the clarity of the mind/body/spirit through which unfolding takes place. When the person is well maintained and nurtured, free of major conflicts, free of distortions and negative conditioning, that person has the greatest opportunity to unfold in a natural and orderly way. Energy will vibrate freely throughout the body and the unconscious seed will blossom more fully.

A View to the Future

We cannot change the nature of the unfolding seeds of our own potential or of the potentials of our clients and patients, but we can influence the vibrations in the subtle body and the media through which life events unfold. Just as the internal preparation of the yogi facilitates the ease of the chakral openings, harmonizing and balancing the vibrations in the subtle body serves a similar function in relation to the behavior manifesting from the blossoming seed of the unconscious.

Through knowledge and skills related to body energies and the inner bridges, we can be of service to ourselves and others in the unfolding of the life process.

Bibliography

General

Arnstein, Robert E. *The Psychology of Consciousness.* San Diego. Harcourt, Brace, Jovanovich, Inc. 1972.

Assagioli, Roberto, M.D. *Psychosynthesis: A Manual of Principles and Techniques.* Psychosynthesis Research Foundation. 1965.

Benson, Herbert, M.D. *The Relaxation Response.* New York. Avon Books. 1974.

Bentof, Itzhak. *Stalking the Wild Pendulum: On the Mechanics of Consciousness.* New York. Bantam Books. 1977.

Bertherat, Therese, and Carol Bernstein. *The Body Has Its Reasons: Anti-exercise and Self Awareness.* New York. Avon Books. 1976.

Brodsky, Greg. *From Eden to Aquarius: The Book of Natural Healing.* New York. Bantam Books. 1974.

Campbell, Joseph. *The Mythic Image.* Princeton, N.J. Princeton University Press. 1974.

Capra, Fritjof. *The Tao of Physics.* Boulder, Colorado. Shambhala Publications. 1975.

Capra, Fritjof. *The Turning Point: Science, Society and the Rising Culture.* New York. Simon & Schuster, Inc. 1982.

Cyrlax, James. *Textbook of Orthopædic Medicine, Vol II: Treatment by Manipulation, Massage and Injection.* Baltimore. Williams & Wilkins. 1944. Eighth Edition, 1971.

Gray, Henry, F.R.S. *Anatomy of the Human Body.* Philadelphia. Lea & Febiger. 1948.

Hulme, Kathryn. *Undiscovered Country: In Search of Gurdjieff.* Boston. Little, Brown & Company, Inc. 1966.

Jampolsky, Gerald G., M.D. *Love Is Letting Go of Fear.* New York. Bantam Books. 1979.

xiJoy, W. Brugh, M.D. *Joy's Way: A Map for the Transformational Journey.* Los Angeles. J.P. Tarcher, Inc. 1978.

Jung, Carl G. *Man and His Symbols.* New York. Doubleday & Co. 1964.

Kapandji, I.A. *The Physiology of the Joints*. Three Volumes. New York. Churchill Livingstone. 1974.

Karagulla, Shafica, M.D. *Breakthrough to Creativity*. Marina del Ray, California. De Vorss & Co., Inc. 1967. Seventh Printing, 1973.

Kervran, Louis C. *Biological Transmutations*. Binghamton, N.Y. Swan House Publishing Co. 1972.

Leonard, George. *The Silent Pulse: A Search for the Perfect Rhythm That Exists in Each of Us*. New York. E.P. Dutton. 1978.

Lockhart, R.D. *Living Anatomy*. London. Faber and Faber, Ltd. First Edition, 1948. Seventh Edition, 1974.

McMennell, John, M.D. *Back Pain: Diagnosis and Treatment Using Manipulative Techniques*. Boston. Little, Brown & Co. 1960.

McMennell, John, M.D. *Joint Pain: Diagnosis and Treatment Using Manipulative Techniques*. Boston. Little, Brown & Co. 1964.

Michell, John. *The Earth Spirit: Its Ways, Shrines and Mysteries*. New York. Avon Books. 1975.

Mishlove, Jeffery. *The Roots of Consciousness: Psychic Liberation Through History, Science and Experience*. New York. Random House. 1975.

Nakamura, Takashi. *Oriental Breathing Therapy*. Tokyo. Japan Publications, Inc. 1981.

Oyle, Dr. Irving. *The Healing Mind: You Can Cure Yourself Without Drugs*. Berkeley, California. Celestial Arts. 1971.

Postle, Denis. *The Fabric of the Universe*. New York. Crown Publishers. 1976.

Samuels, Mike, M.D., and Nancy Samuels. *Seeing with the Mind's Eye*. New York. Random House. 1975.

Schauberger, Viktor. *Living Water*. (The Secrets of Natural Energy by Olof Alexandersson.) Northamptonshire, England. Turnstone Press, Ltd. 1982.

Schwartz ,J.S. *Human Energy Systems*. New York. E.P. Dutton. 1980.

Schwenk, Theodor. *Sensitive Chaos: The Creation of Flowing Forms in Water and Air*. New York. Rudolf Steiner Press, 1965. Schocken Books, 1978.

Tiller, William A. "Creating a New Functional Model of Body Healing," *Journal of Holistic Health* IV. 1979.

Tiller, William A. *Towards a Future Medicine Based on Controlled Energy Fields*. Stanford, California. Phoenex Vol 1, No. 1, Summer, 1977.

Tiller, William A. *The Simulator and the Being*. Stanford, California. Phoenex Vol. 1, No. 2, Fall/Winter, 1977.

Tiller, William A. *Radionics, Radiesthesia and Physics*. Academy of Parapsychology and Medicine Symposium Transcript, The Varieties of Healing Experiences. Oct., 1971.

Tiller, William A. "Toward a Scientific Rationale of Homeopathy." *Journal of Homeopathic Practice* II, No. 2, 1979.

Tiller, William A. "Two Space-Time Mirror-like Universes: Some Consequences for Humanity." *Phoenex* Vol. 2, No. 1,1978.

Todd, Mabel Elsworth. *The Thinking Body: A Study of the Balancing Forces of Dynamic Man*. Paul Hoeber, Inc. 1937.

Tulku, Tarthang. *Gesture of Balance: A Guide to Awareness, Self-Healing and Meditation.* Dharama Publishing. 1977.

Vithoulkas, George. *The Science of Homeopathy.* New York. Grove Press. 1980.

Zukaw, Gay. *The Dancing Wu Li Masters: An Overview of the New Physics.* New York. William Morrow and Co., Inc. 1919.

Acupuncture

Academy of Traditional Chinese Medicine. *Essentials of Chinese Acupuncture.* Bejing. Foreign Languages Press. 1980.

Academy of Traditional Chinese Medicine. *An Outline of Chinese Acupuncture.* Peking. Foreign Languages Press. 1975.

Austin, Dr. Mary. *Acupuncture Therapy.* New York. ASI Publishers, Inc. 1972.

Hashimoto, Mme. Dr. H. *Japanese Acupuncture.* Edited and annotated by Dr. Philip M. Chancellor. New York. Liveright Publishing Corp. 1968.

Low, Royston. *The Secondary Vessels of Acupuncture.* Wellingborough, Northamptonshire, England. Thorsons Publishers, Ltd.1983.

Mann, Felix, M.B. *Acupuncture: The Ancient Chinese Art of Healing.* New York. Vintage Books. 1972.

McGarey, William A. M.D. *Acupuncture and Body Energies.* Phoenix, AZ. Gabriel Press. 1974.

Moss, Louis, M.D. *Acupuncture and You.* New York. Citadel Press. 1966.

O'Connor, John, and Dan Bensky (trans.). *Acupuncture: A Comprehensive Text.* Shanghai College of Traditional Medicine. Seattle. Eastland Press. 1982.

Porkert, Manfred. *The Theoretical Foundations of Chinese Medicine: Systems of Correspondence.* Cambridge, Mass.; London, England. MIT Press. 1974.

Veith, Ilza. *The Yellow Emperor's Classic of Internal Medicine.* Berkeley. University of California Press. 1972.

Woolerton, Henry, and Colleen J. McLean. *Acupuncture Energy in Health and Disease: A Practical Guide for Advanced Students.* Northamptonshire, England. Thorsons Publishers, Ltd. 1979.

Yu-Min Chuang, Dr. *Chinese Acupuncture.* Translated by Desmond K. Shiu. New York. Oriental Publications. 1972.

Health

Airola, Paavo. *Are You Confused?* Phoenix, Arizona. Health Plus Publishers. 1971.

Airola, Paavo. *How to Get Well.* Phoenix, Arizona. Health Plus Publishers. First printing, 1974. Fifteenth printing, 1979.

Cousins, Norman. *Anatomy of an Illness.* New York. W.W. Norton & Co. 1979.

Gesser, Charles H. *The Principles of Natural Living and Natural Healing.* Tampa, Fla. Gesser Publications. 1966.

Johnson, J. Stanley, Jr., M.D., BAc. *To My Patients.* J. Stanley Johnson, Jr. 1977.

Sanford, John A. *Healing and Wholeness.* New York. Paulist Press, 1977.

Simonton, Carl, M.D. *Getting Well Again.* New York. Bantam Books.

Turner, Roger Newman. *Naturopathic Medicine: Treating the Whole Person.* Northamptonshire, England. Thorsons Publishers, Ltd.

Yoga

Chia, Mantak. *Awaken Healing Energy Through the Tao.* 205 3rd Ave. Second, N.Y. 1983.

Karanjia, R.K. *Kundalini Yoga.* 10 East 39th Street, N.Y. Kundalini Research Foundation. 1977.

Krishna, Gopi. *The Awakening of Kundalini.* New York. Kundalini Research Foundation. 1975.

Krishna, Pandit Gopi. *The Secret of Yoga.* New York & London. Harper & Row.

Mishra, Rammurti S., M.D. *The Textbook of Yoga Psychology.* New York. Julian Press, Inc. 1963.

Motoyama, Hiroshi. *Theories of the Chakras. Bridge to Higher Consciousness.* A Quest Book., Illinois. Theosophical Publishing House. 1981.

Muktananda, Swami. *Kundalini: The Secret of Life.* South Fallsburg, N.Y. SYDA Foundation.

Rama, Swami. *Voluntary Control Project.* Topeka, Kansas. Research Department, Menninger Foundation.

Rama, Swami, Rudolph Ballentine, M.D., and Swami Ajaya, Ph.D. *Yoga and Psychotherapy: The Evolution of Consciousness.* Pennsylvania. Himalayan International Institute of Yoga Science and Philosophy. 1976.

Ramacharaka, Yogi. *Fourteen Lessons in Yogi Philosophy.* London. Yogi Publication Society. 1911.

Sannella, Lee, M.D. *Kundalini: Psychosis or Transcendence.* San Francisco. H.S. Dakin Co. 1976.

Vishnudevananda, Swami. *The Complete Illustrated Book of Yoga.* New York. Julian Press, Inc. 1960.

Woodroffe, Sir John. *The Serpent Power.* Madras 17, India. Garnesh & Co. First Edition, 1918. Tenth Edition, 1974.

Yogananda, Paramahansa. *Autobiography of a Yogi.* Los Angeles. Self-Realization Fellowship. Copyright, 1946. Tenth Edition, 1971.

Index

About the Author

Fritz Frederick Smith, M.D., graduated from the College of Osteopathic Physicians and Surgeons in 1955 and from the California College of Medicine in 1961. He holds bachelor and masters degrees from the College of Chinese Medicine (in the United Kingdom). He is a Cranial Osteopath, Certified Rolfer (inactive), California Certified Acupuncturist, approved examiner for the California Acupuncture Examination, and board member and former senior faculty member of the Traditional Acupuncture Institute in Columbia, Maryland.

Dr. Smith is the founder of the Zero Balancing system, a structural acupressure system. Formerly in general practice, he now limits his practice to Traditional Chinese Acupuncture, Osteopathic Manipulation, and Zero Balancing.

Elizabeth McBride Smith